When the Church Burns Down, Cancel the Wedding

Adventures from the Other Half of Single

D1109045

Sara E. Braca

NEW DEGREE PRESS

COPYRIGHT © 2022 SARA E. BRACA

WHEN THE CHURCH BURNS DOWN, CANCEL THE WEDDING
Adventures from the Other Half of Single

This book is a memoir. It reflects the author's present recollections of events and experiences that have been relayed to the best of the author's knowledge. Some names and identities have been changed or are composites, and some dialogue has been recreated.

ISBN

979-8-88504-598-8   *Paperback*

979-8-88504-945-0   *Kindle Ebook*

979-8-88504-832-3   *Digital Ebook*

WHEN THE CHURCH BURNS DOWN, CANCEL THE WEDDING

For Nettie and Daddy,

and the memories preserved in these pages

Anche per il mio capo, Lou

Contents

Author's Note 9

Altars Ablaze! 15
Meeting Michael Bublé 23
That Moment in Amsterdam 33
Switzerland via Snowplow 45
My Heart Belongs to Santorini 55
Bosses, Budgets, and Bikinis 69
The Inadvertent Tupperware Party 79
International Yoga 83
Mitzi and the Magic Markets 89
Studies Show, I'm an Asshole 103
Through the Water Glass 111
Dead Sea Diving 117
Kept Women in Umbria 129
The Revelation of Naples 143
The Empath and the Sommelier 153
Meet-Cute Meltdown 161
Late Night Algarve 175
Iceland: The (Christmas) Cat's Meow 189
The Other Half of Single 203
Epilogue 211

Acknowledgments 213
Appendix 217
About the Author 219

Author's Note

———

I have always hated writing.

I am not entirely sure why, but I imagine it's some combination of my excessive perfectionism and need for a clear final answer that has made writing my life's nemesis. I wrote my entire college application essay about this deep and abiding writing aversion, quoting my own bad high school essays and critiquing them. Somehow, I guess this raw honesty was appealing, and I was accepted into Dartmouth. I later learned that this ridiculous essay turned an otherwise solid "maybe" application into a compelling yes.

From the first moment I set foot on Dartmouth's campus, I knew I was going to be a math major. I had done my research; this was the only degree I could earn that would not require me to write a thesis. After college, I became a banker (no writing). When that got too soul-crushing, I got an MBA, where I was a finance TA for fun, and a marketing and operations double major (still no writing!). This ultimately led to my current career in brand management. While this is a marginally more creative career than banking, still almost no real writing is involved; that's what advertising agencies are for. In my everyday life, "writing" consists of writing emails in which I use business phrases to evaluate the work of actual copywriters. It's pretty glorious.

So, imagine my surprise when, in the months before my fortieth birthday, I suddenly decided I wanted to write a book to share my unintentionally counterculture perspective with the world. Specifically, I am happily single, a solo adventurer with a talent for finding joy in unexpected places. And it seems that living my life this way causes a strange mixture of surprise, inspiration, and disdain from others.

Although singles are one of the fastest growing groups in the United States—according to the US Census Bureau, 28 percent of all US households are single, up from 13 percent in 1960—society doesn't seem to know what to make of us. Whenever I travel alone, nice couples in restaurants call me brave for eating by myself. Women of all ages tell me they wish they could travel solo and are inspired to see me doing it. A harried mom once stopped me in an amusement park to say that she'd never seen anyone alone look as happy as I did. I'm still not sure if that was a compliment or not.

Certainly, not everyone is supportive. I'm regularly asked why I am "still" single, as if "single" is such a miserable state that I should be on a constant quest to exit it. My equal-parts healthy and dramatic Italian American mother tells me often, with a lingering sigh, that she doesn't want to die knowing I am *still* alone.

While more people are choosing to stay single, the social norms that demonize single-hood are holding strong. It often feels like everyone around the world expects a single person like me to be home alone crying into my cat, and they are collectively shocked to see another way of living standing enthusiastically in front of them.

To be honest, navigating singledom hasn't always been sunshine and rainbows. After my divorce, it was pretty terrifying figuring everything out alone after nearly a decade of living partnered. With time, lots of trial and error, and many embarrassing "learning" moments (just ask Michael Bublé), I realized I was so much stronger than I had ever imagined and there's no one-size-fits-all model for a happy life. The net result of the mixed reactions of others and my own life experiences prompted a quest—not to end my single status (sorry, Mom), but to celebrate it. My life proves that I don't need to be partnered to be happy, and I started thinking that writing a book would be a way to share my hard-fought perspective with more people than the few I ran into on my adventures. Imagine the positive impact on the world if more of this growing population of singletons could feel empowered to live fully now and not feel like they had to wait for a partner for their lives to begin!

So, I found myself with a rather baffling internal conflict. I had something to say and part of me wanted to write a book to say it. The rest of me considered my thirty-nine-year history of writing misery and subsequent writing-avoidant behavior and concluded that the aspiring-writer part had gone completely bat-shit crazy. Convinced that my midlife crisis was about to become a psychotic break, I took a trip to my favorite place in the world, Santorini, the Greek island, to clear my head. Obviously, I couldn't write a book. The mere thought of writing anything more than an email on purpose sent cold shivers of dread down my spine, kind of like that feeling when you stupidly watch *Dateline* at home alone on a Friday night during a thunderstorm while even your cat has enough sense to hide under the sofa.

I went to my favorite bookstore, the only one on the island, in search of a distraction from these persistent book-writing thoughts, which, in retrospect, was rather ironic—to seek books in an attempt to avoid writing one. They have this funky table of books that the staff recommends. For the record, both the table itself and the books on it are funky; everything about this shop is funky. Entry requires passage down a violently steep and winding flight of stairs. The shop is full to bursting of people, books, cats, and weird dangling signs that hit you in the head as you try to shop. I love it.

On the funky table was a book titled *The Opposite of Loneliness* by Marina Keegan. The cover art showed this brazen-looking young woman, who seemed tough and smart and on a mission. She looked like a badass, the title sounded interesting, and it was recommended by the staff, so I picked it up. It's kind of funny how a little decision like picking up a book in a funky bookstore can change the course of your life. Marina was a Yale student and a promising writer on staff at the *Yale Daily News*. She was about to start her career as a professional writer when she was tragically killed in a car accident a week after her college graduation. She was twenty-two years old.

Here I was, thirty-nine years old, lamenting my old age and the passage of time, trying to convince myself that I had no stories to tell and that I couldn't write them if I did. And here was this woman, full of stories, who had all that potential taken from her. She never made it to twenty-three. I felt as if the entire Universe shook me violently and shouted, "Pay attention!" This woman couldn't tell her stories anymore, but I could still tell mine. Given my history of ignoring signs from the Universe—most notably, the fire that burned down the church one week before my ill-fated wedding—I knew in that moment I needed to listen to this one. That night, I went back to my hotel and wrote my first ever non-graded, on-purpose, not-an-email story.

What follows is a collection of my stories—starting from that fateful fire, crisscrossing the globe, bringing me to the next big leap, where I sit now in my fifteenth-century apartment in Tuscany after a solo (okay, my cat came, too), transcontinental move. These stories are a true labor of love for the past many months of my life. I'm still amazed that they exist and that I actually wrote them. And also that, even though my life really didn't go the way I thought it would when I was twenty-two, I wouldn't change a thing—except maybe for that night with the stunning Portuguese sommelier.

Anyway, I hope you enjoy my stories. If not, I hope you'll remember I was a math major.

Altars Ablaze!

———

It was my last day at work before my wedding, a little more than a week before the Big Day. Between Christmas, the wedding, and my honeymoon in Tahiti, I was planning to be out of the office for nearly four weeks and was trying to stay focused on wrapping up my projects so I could enjoy my time away when my desk phone rang. I was surprised to see my mom's name on the caller ID. My mom never called my office; I didn't think she even knew my office phone number. And why would she be calling me when she knew how much work I needed to finish? Slightly alarmed, I answered the phone.

"Hi, Sara." She sounded quiet and nervous, neither of which are adjectives that have ever been used to describe my mother. Something was definitely wrong.

"What's wrong?"

"Well, it's just the church," she said, stammering. My mother does not stammer.

"What about the church?" My voice was hitting a higher pitch.

"Well, there was a small fire. . ."

"*What?*" My cube mates turned away from their screens and stared at me.

"Well, you know how Father Nick likes to decorate the church with all the trees and lights? This year, it was so beautiful. He had so many trees! And you should have seen how beautiful the altar looked."

I noticed she was speaking in the past tense.

"So, last night, one of the extension cords shorted out from all the Christmas lights and there was a fire."

"Okay." I was trying to sound calm. I mean, how bad could a fire caused by Christmas lights be? "How bad was the fire?"

"Well, your uncle was driving past the church last night and saw the smoke and then waited and saw the fire trucks come. He called me when he got home and said that there were fire trucks. I tried to call Father Nick, but you know how busy he is."

What? "How bad was the fire, Mom?"

"Well, there were fire trucks . . . so I called the president of the Ladies Guild." She wasn't making any sense.

"How bad was it, Mom?"

"Well, I finally reached Father Nick, and he said that the altar, and well, pretty much the whole interior of the church was kind of destroyed and the church will be closed for about nine or ten months."

Did I mention that my wedding was just over a week away? Or, more specifically, my wedding scheduled to be in the now-burned-down church was just over a week away?

"Whaaaat?"

"Well, there was a wedding this weekend, honey. It could be worse."

I think I was now hyperventilating. My colleagues had formed a semicircle around my cube. I had been planning my wedding for almost two years. Lots of things had changed and morphed throughout the planning process, but the one constant was the church. The plan had always been to get married at the church where I had grown up, and the one thing I was most looking forward to was how beautiful the church looked during the holidays. Father Nick had a great eye for design, if not electrical engineering.

Luckily, Mom had a plan.

My hometown in Connecticut is generally pretty eclectic. *The New York Times* recently described it as "part suburb, part historic village, part gritty downtown, part industrial complex, part commercial corridor, part open space." As diverse as it may be in terms of lifestyle options, it's strangely homogenous when it comes to religion. According to Best Places to Live, more than 70 percent of residents who identify as religious also identify as Catholic. Growing up, I felt like everyone I knew in town was Catholic. I think this was because so many of my classmates were first- or second-generation Americans like me—the children and grandchildren of European immigrants. I had little appreciation for the fact that the rest of the world included people who were not Catholic European American immigrants until I went away to college.

But anyway, there was a benefit to living in an all-Catholic town: When your Catholic church burns down the week before your wedding, you can move your wedding to one of several other Catholic churches in town. So that's what my mom and I did. We called the other Catholic churches, found the one that could accommodate the rest of the wedding-day schedule, and moved the wedding. Then, I called all 125 guests and told them about the changes:

"Hi [Insert Wedding Guest Name Here], it's Sara."

"Hi Sara! Why are you calling me? You must be going crazy with the last-minute wedding details!"

"Well, that's actually why I'm calling. There was a fire at St. Lawrence and we are moving the wedding to St. Joseph's."

"What do you mean? There was a fire in the church?"

"It was the Christmas lights."

"Why do such crazy things always happen to you?"

"I've been asking myself that for years."

The consistency of that last point was pretty noteworthy. Crazy situations and inexplicable events had always followed me around. I don't think I realized this was obvious to other people until every single person I called thought my church burning down the week before my wedding sort of made sense given that it was me and my wedding. I made a mental note to reflect on this from the beach in Tahiti.

The wedding, now at St. Joseph's, went off without a hitch, save for a minor bridezilla freakout about how dark that church was with so few Christmas lights, and a nagging, low-grade but constant nausea that I attributed to wedding-fire-related stress, but which might have actually been my gut trying to tell me something. . .

Six Years Later

"Sara, it's Amy. We have to catch up. It's been too long! Call me!"

"Hey, Sara! It's me again! Why didn't you call me back? Hope you are doing something amazing! Call me! We have to talk!"

"Sara, where are you? Selling ketchup cannot be this consuming! Call me!"

The truth was I had been avoiding Amy. I had been avoiding all of my friends, actually. I was so stunned by the turn of events my life had taken that I couldn't talk about it. I didn't want to say the words aloud.

I was getting divorced.

My husband had had an affair with someone over five years my junior and was leaving me to be with her. I found out when 1-800-Flowers called our house to ask about a flower delivery order—red roses for the other woman—red roses from the man I had been with for nine years, married for six, and who had sent me flowers only once, on our first Valentine's Day together. "Sending flowers is inefficient," he would always tell me. He was an economist; he viewed everything in terms of money and efficiency. "Flowers are too expensive." "The cats will try to eat them, anyway." Yet he had sent roses to this other woman. Ironically, she had cats, too, but I guess not the kind that would try to eat flowers sent from her married boyfriend.

Initially, I didn't believe it was possible that he had actually sent another woman flowers, or that this *meant* something. I came up with all sorts of "rational" explanations. Maybe she had a bad day or suffered some terrible tragedy. It just couldn't be what it sounded like. So, when he got home that night, I asked him about the flowers.

"I got a strange phone call today."

My husband barely acknowledged me as he continued to unpack his bag and followed one of our cats into the living room.

Following him, I continued talking. "It was from 1-800-Flowers."

He looked up slightly from petting the cat.

"They said that they weren't able to deliver the roses you sent to one of your students? What was that all about?"

We both came from very Catholic families. Divorces were nearly unheard of. It just wasn't possible that this meant something. But it did.

His face went grey. He sat down heavily on our new tawny microfiber armchair and started rubbing his eyes, as if to stop seeing the moment that was now happening.

"One of my students was having a bad day yesterday and was telling me about it after the economics club happy hour. And, well, one thing led to another and so I, uh . . . I sent her flowers today."

"One thing led to another?" I repeated back slowly. "What exactly does that mean? What did you do?"

I could hear the pitch of my voice rising, the panic in my words.

"What do you think it means?" he snapped, going from contrite to angry in one sentence. "We slept together."

I don't remember what I said, if I said anything. I know I was standing by the armchair when the conversation began and, somehow, I found myself sitting on the floor, crumpled at his feet, like a servant.

"It's just . . . she's special. I can't explain it. But I think I love her. I feel the same way I felt when I first met you."

I felt my heart explode in my chest. My stomach dropped through the floor as the knife twisted deeper.

"But I don't understand. How could you do this? What about me? Don't you love me?"

"It just happened; I couldn't stop it . . . so, no, I don't think I love you anymore. I don't think I have for a while."

And somehow I found myself crying and hugging him. It was this intense feeling of pure metaphysical confusion— confusion about where to seek comfort when my world was falling apart precisely because of the person from whom I had sought comfort for the past nine years of my life. It was the first of many moments when I felt like the foundation of my being was irreparably cracked and I'd never be solid again.

Not long after, he moved out of our house. The house we had bought not even a year earlier when we both found jobs near the same city, a feat that had required extreme focus given our two divergent careers. The house he insisted we buy when I wanted to rent as we adjusted to a new city. The house where he left his wedding ring, in the kitchen cabinet next to the coffee so he knew I'd see it that morning when I made my coffee like I did every morning. The house he would come back to during the days when I was at work, moving things around and threatening to take my cats, leaving me shaken and paranoid and terrified of what I'd find when I came home at night.

And I had told none of my friends. I was in denial, in shock. How could this charming, handsome man I trusted, whom I thought I'd spend my whole life with, do this to me?

I couldn't keep ignoring Amy's calls, though. Amy wasn't the kind of person you could ignore. A passionate feminist and certified self-defense instructor trainer—yes, she *trains* self-defense instructors—Amy is a force of nature. She was likely one more missed call away from filing a missing person's report. So, when she called again that night, I had to pick up.

"Where have you been?" she shouted at me when I answered the phone. "I was literally about to call the police!"

Somehow, I managed to tell her what was going on. After a long silence, which was strange because Amy also doesn't do silence, she finally started talking and said the best thing anyone has ever said to me in my entire life:

"Sara, the next time you decide to get married, and God *burns down the church*, promise me you'll call it off. Will you?"

For the first time in what felt like an eternity, I laughed. The sound of my own laughter, a sound I wasn't certain I'd hear again, was the most reassuring sound I'd ever heard. It was the glimmer of hope I needed. If I could laugh despite all the pain and loneliness and sadness I was mired in, maybe I could find some light at the end of this long tunnel? And I resolved at that moment to take Amy's advice.

Meeting Michael Bublé

To understand what happens to my emotions when I've bottled them up for too long, try dropping a bottle of champagne . . . from a skyscraper.

Or just ask Michael Bublé.

Several years before the infamous call from 1-800-Flowers, I relocated to the Richmond, Virginia, area to accommodate my husband's budding career and was not loving life. I felt uprooted, in a new city where I knew no one, and increasingly resentful. For his part, my husband was totally preoccupied with his new job. It was like he had a full life—a career he loved, friends from work, the support of a partner—and my needs were an afterthought. Of course, I wasn't willing to acknowledge this at the time and instead attributed my misery to work, which was at least partially valid.

I had given up an impressive-sounding banking job in Washington, DC, and was now a financial analyst at an insurance company, a demanding and unfulfilling job that I loathed. This kind of loathing had me waking up with a pit in my stomach every morning and wanting to punch nice people at parties when they asked me what I did for a living. I had decided I needed to make a career change to avoid stomach ulcers and jail time, and the only way to do that was to go back to business school for my MBA.

Since business school is commonly viewed as an all-access pass to wealth, connections, and opportunities, the barriers to entry are very high. Standardized testing, essays, interviews—it felt like a full-time job on top of my actual day job. But given this perception of business school, and the generally bad reputation of business school students—i.e., aspiring financiers who would step on their own mothers for more money and influence—the stress I was under was not exactly something I could share with others, even my husband, without looking like a petulant brat. In my defense, I wanted to go to business school to get *out* of finance and *into* marketing, and everyone knows marketers are less objectionable than bankers, but still. I was in a miserable place, doing miserable work, spending my "free" time in application misery and couldn't complain to anyone. At this point, Michael Bublé entered the picture.

On my way to my hideous job one morning, I was listening to the radio when the deejay gave me the ray of hope I needed to get through another awful day. Michael Bublé would be coming to Richmond as part of his tour, and the radio station was running a contest. Write an essay about why you deserved to meet Michael Bublé, and you could win a meet and greet with him before his concert! This announcement felt like the light at the end of the tunnel!

I was a Michael Bublé super fan, a card-carrying member of his fan club. I listened to his music obsessively and would regale friends with endless rhapsodies about how amazing and talented and perfect he was. In a pretty miserable time of my life, channeling my energy into Michael Bublé's brand of feel-good escapism was my saving grace—and, in retrospect, probably exacerbated the growing cracks in my marriage. How could any husband live up to Michael Bublé?

I had a small problem, though. Writing hadn't been easy for me historically, which was a supreme understatement. I'd long believed that eternal essay writing would qualify as a punishment worthy of one of Dante's layers of hell. At the time this essay contest was announced, I was already in essay-writing hell for my graduate school applications. So, I procrastinated. The night before the essay was due, I had typed my name in a Word document. I realized I had to write something; I would never forgive myself if I didn't at least try. This is what I came up with—very clearly not my best work:

"I am the best person to meet Michael Bublé because I am currently an incredibly stressed-out perfectionist in dire need of Michael's unique brand of escapism!

First, let me say that I am a huge fan of Michael and his music. I discovered him several years ago and listen to his music incessantly. I also had the opportunity to see Michael in concert last year and it was one of the most amazing experiences of my life. In addition to his music, I love his humor and charm, and the fact that he seems to be a genuinely kind person. I would relish the chance to thank him for making such beautiful music and for showing that men can be strong, sexy and talented, as well as emotional and compassionate. But I am sure everyone entering this contest would agree with me on these points. The more unique element of this essay is that I credit Michael with helping me survive the graduate business school application process. Right now, I am waiting rather impatiently to find out if/where I will be going to school this fall and meeting Michael would be the most perfect gift and welcome distraction that I can imagine!

The application process for business school is excruciating and lasts many agonizing months. The first step is to take the GMAT, the standardized test required for business school admissions. A high score on this test is critical. While taking the verbal section of this test, I encountered a reading passage that I maintain was not actually English. Seconds away from panic and abject GMAT failure, "Feeling Good" popped into my head. The irony of that song in the midst of my preparations to commit hari-kari struck me as funny and thinking about Michael's fabulous opening performance of that song during his concert made me grin from ear-to-ear (and possibly drool a bit). Distracted from my panic, the test ended up a success and I am grateful to Michael for his unintentional help.

After the GMAT, I wrote twenty-one essays, discovered that perfectionists trying to write twenty-one reasonable essays while working full-time can function on remarkably little sleep, engaged in significant hand wringing about my relative worth, concluded that "hand wringing" should be considered a viable alternative to the elliptical machine, consumed vast amounts of coffee (Starbucks, of course!) and finally submitted five applications in early January to schools in cities across the US. Michael's CDs and DVDs were my constant companions and stress reducers during this time (and also the only items in existence able to tolerate my incessant hand wringing). In January, I also learned about Michael's tour schedule and bought tickets to see him in both Washington, DC, and Richmond. (Last week, I couldn't resist the temptation and bought tickets to Norfolk as well!) I spent all of February interviewing at the schools where I applied and now I'm just waiting, hoping, and praying for a good outcome. I seriously underestimated the stress of waiting. I find myself with lots of time to think about the fact that I have no idea where I'll be living in five months and that the process is completely out of my hands. In fact, every time the cell phone rings or my email buzzes, I suffer a minor coronary. The only thing preserving my sanity is Michael's music (ever-present in my car and on my iPod) and knowing that I will soon see him live!

This year, I set two New Year's resolutions for myself: to get accepted into a strong business graduate school program and to meet Michael Bublé. While these may seem objectively like rather disparate goals, as you can see, they are actually quite related in my mind. While I doubt you can influence the business schools as they make their decisions, I truly hope you will give me the chance to achieve my goal of meeting Michael!"

Yikes.

Well, in marketing, we talk a lot about the value of being "single-minded" and focused, and this essay is certainly that— except that I was single-mindedly sharing that I was a crazed fanatic. Seeing him in concert was "one of the most amazing experiences of my life"? That begs the obvious question, what was I doing with my life? How on earth would I know that he is "emotional and compassionate"? And let me tell you about how I have tickets to basically every stop on his concert tour. I can't believe anyone would let me meet this dude given how delusional and stalker-ish this all sounds.

Also, did I realize what hari-kari was when I wrote this? Dictionary.com defines it as "ceremonial suicide by ripping open the abdomen with a dagger or knife: formerly practiced in Japan by members of the warrior class when disgraced or sentenced to death." Um, *wow*. That seems like an extreme reaction to a standardized test. And I spelled it wrong; it's supposed to be *hara-kiri*. Possibly most offensive is the blatant pandering with the Starbucks reference since Michael Bublé was in a Starbucks commercial. This is appalling because I actually think Starbucks coffee is vile; I'm a Dunkin' girl, thank you very much. I will give myself some credit for the strong, if completely ludicrous, close. I mean, how could someone not want to help a smart, deluded woman achieve her New Year's resolution?

Whatever. I decided to release myself from my harsh but fair criticisms and just be happy-ish that I had submitted something. At least I tried.

The week of the concert arrived. I was planning to go to the concert with a colleague since my husband wasn't interested in joining me, but I had lost hope about actually meeting Michael Bublé. I was at work, immersed in a spreadsheet when my phone rang. I sat in a cubicle in the middle of the floor, and the whole area was always deadly silent. It was as if all of us cubicle dwellers were in silent mourning for our miserable existences. When I answered my phone, I was expecting more unclear direction from my micromanaging boss. However, that was not to be.

"Hi, I'm calling from the radio station and looking for Sara Braca."

Oh. My. God.

"Um, I'm Sara." I was talking super quietly, as was custom in the Cubicle Bank of Sorrows.

"So, we loved your essay and want to see if you would like to meet Michael Bublé on Thursday night?"

"Yes, oh my God, *yes!*" I screamed into my phone (Cubicle Bank of Sorrows, be damned). Cube dwellers' heads were popping up over their cube half-walls, possibly wondering if Jesus had returned to save us from our lives of misery.

The radio station lady told me all the details, which I repeated like eight times back to her at a higher and higher pitch each time, to the point where only dogs could understand my excited squeals. When I got off the phone, I realized that my concert-going colleague was standing outside my cube—one never, ever enters someone's cube without permission, even if that person appears to be having a hysterical fit—summoned by the cacophony of squealing coming from my cube. We immediately finalized our plan: Do an *Office Space*-style escape as early as we could that evening and buy new outfits for the concert. Repeat escape the night of the concert with fancy new outfits.

So, the day of the concert arrived. I was calmer, had an awesome new outfit to wear, and had started to think about what I would actually say when the amazing Michael Bublé was standing in front of me. I realized my reaction with the radio station lady wasn't exactly cool. And I wanted Michael Bublé to think I was cool. The conundrum: How could I convey to Michael Bublé that I was cute and charming and witty and not a psychopath in a few sentences? Seemed to me that I needed a mantra, so I chose this: "You are a smart, professional woman." Clearly, a smart, professional woman would handle herself in a cool manner when meeting a sexy celebrity musician. I practiced what I would say to Michael Bublé: "Michael [a cool, smart, professional woman would use his first name, right?], I just love your music. You are so talented. Thank you for doing what you do!" I said this in front of the mirror to make sure I looked as cool as I wanted to be when I said it.

We arrived at the concert early and were sent to a big room backstage. Eight other people were there. Two were from the production company and part of the Michael Bublé team. One was an executive from a local music-related company and his wife. The four others were radio station people, not necessarily Michael Bublé super fans like me and my friend. They all seemed calm, like this wasn't the most exciting moment in their lives. So, I repeated my mantra in my head. "You are a smart, professional woman."

And then Michael Bublé walked into the room. I was at the end of the line to meet him, so I excitedly watched him charm all the others in the group. And then, after what seemed like an eternity, he got to me and my friend. Suddenly, I found myself jumping up and down, shrieking, "*Oh my God! Oh my God! Oh my God!*" Jumping up and down. I could not stop my feet from jumping. I could not stop my mouth from shrieking. I realized no one else was doing this, but I couldn't stop. And then, in a shocking moment of mental clarity, I realized that a latent thirteen-year-old teeny bopper had been released from her smart, professional woman prison the second Michael Bublé had said hello. But still, my feet kept jumping! Michael Bublé turned to (completely crazed) me and grabbed my hands and started jumping up and down with me, shrieking, "*Oh my God! Oh my God! Oh my God!*" back to me. So, for an indeterminate amount of time, Michael Bublé and I held hands, jumped up and down together, and shouted, "*Oh my God!*" in each other's faces. Somehow, this calmed me down and I eventually stopped jumping and shrieking. Finally, I regained the power of speech.

"I'm so thrilled to meet you! I love your music! I really can't believe this!" The words were close to what I had planned to say, but I obviously did not achieve "cool" given the aforementioned jumping incident.

Michael Bublé—clearly teasing me, doing that thing little kids do when they are nervous, with their knees knocking together and their ankles out—said, "I'm so excited to meet *you!*" And then, more seriously, "Thanks for coming."

"Can I hug you?" Radio station lady was probably *really* regretting picking me as contest winner by now.

At some point, someone took a photo of Michael Bublé, my friend and me, so there is visual proof of this awesomely catastrophic night. I don't recall the photo-taking as much as the entire rest of the group circling me once Michael left and trying to get me to resume breathing.

The moral of this story? Beware of the teeny bopper within. Or perhaps: Do not meet your favorite celebrity when you are a crazed super fan under a lot of stress and on the brink of divorce? Even better: When it's time to open the champagne, hold the bottle firmly and rotate it slowly, nudging the cork out with a delicate pop to release the sparkliness with care.

That Moment in
Amsterdam

———

The best advice is always the hardest advice to take.
"I've listened to you complain and feel sorry for yourself for months, but you need to realize that you have a choice.
A bad thing happened to you. Are you going to let that one
bad thing make you miserable for the rest of your life? It's
up to you. Do you really want to spend the rest of your life
being bitter?"

I didn't want to admit it, but my therapist had a point.

We all know those bitter, man-hating divorced women.
Someone did them very wrong at some point in their lives, and
they never let it or him go. They're the ones glaring at young
couples in love, commenting snarkily at weddings, and making
every happily partnered person around them uncomfortable,
all while secretly researching their exes and looking for signs
that they are missed. I was well on my way to becoming one
of those women about six months after my husband left.

I had good reason to be angry. I had supported my husband for most of our time together, working at jobs I detested

and moving around the country to places I never wanted to live to enable his budding career, only to be left for a woman more than five years my junior just as I was starting to find my groove career-wise.

To make matters worse, I had lost myself in my marriage. Over time, I had lost touch with anyone my husband didn't like, which was pretty much all of my friends and most of my family. I lost my confidence as I grew more and more dependent on him and his friends. I lost my passions as I stopped doing many of the things that mattered most to me, even traveling less to appease his worries about being away from home for too long and spending too much money. I felt like I had devoted my twenties to supporting his dreams and now I was thirty-one and alone and terrified.

Adding insult to injury, my ex-husband is an economics professor, and economics as an academic discipline is one of the most boring things on earth. The real reason why it's called the dismal science: It's awful. So "supporting his career" meant dedicating my time and efforts to painstakingly reading and editing his writing, which meant I had to read about economics in the process. I can't tell you how many times I nearly jabbed my pen in my eye to justify not editing his latest boring essay about eternal boringness. He wrote an entire book; it was absolute torture. And these years of unintentionally studying economics have stuck. I still, to this day, will find myself wondering about the "market clearing price" of an item when I'm shopping, which is incredibly irritating. (According to Investopedia, the market clearing price is the price at which the demand for a good equals the amount of goods that can be produced at that price.) In retrospect, I'd probably have been less angry had he been a professor of nearly anything else. At least I could've learned something cool pre-heartbreak.

But, anyway, I had a choice to make. I was doing a great job at being bitter. But I also really hate being around bitter, depressing people who suck the energy out of a room. A woman I knew in college was like this; she'd walk into a room and everyone's energy level would drop. I nicknamed her "Gravity" because she brought everyone down around her. And I once worked with a guy I thought of as the "Great Deflator," a nice person, but impossibly draining to be around for long. Every meeting with him made me want to call my therapist; I tried to avoid him.

Even beyond the effect I anticipated that my negative self would have on others, I was afraid of what this would mean for me. I didn't want to wake up sad every morning, wondering what was wrong with me and wishing things were different. I knew I couldn't change the past, but I understood that the future wasn't yet written. It was the most terrible time in my life. I felt caught between worlds and realities. I didn't like or want my current reality, I couldn't get my old one back, and I wasn't able to process any other options. I just knew I needed to make a change, but I didn't know how to do that, either. I felt lost.

"Why don't you take a trip?" asked a friend with the slightly raised eyebrows and calm, overly measured tone of someone trying to be helpful while simultaneously blocking the path to the ledge.

Since one of my biggest complaints about my husband was his lack of interest in traveling, that seemed like a logical place to start. So, I called my friends, looking for a travel partner. This turned out to be a much harder task than I was anticipating. I was struck by the inverse relationship between money and time when it comes to travel. When I was younger, I had lots of time but no money to travel. As I got older, I had more money but no time. When I was in college and studying abroad, it was so easy to find friends to travel with; we had all the time in the world and were really only limited by funding. Women in their early thirties are busy with careers and new husbands and new babies. I was busy, too, with a demanding job and limited vacation time, and I couldn't find any friends whose schedules and interests aligned with mine. My plan looked like it was going to fail before it even started.

"Why don't you just travel alone?" asked the same well-meaning friend.

I thought she was insane. The mere idea of solo travel absolutely terrified me. Wouldn't I be lonely by myself in a strange place? I envisioned an unintentional, but self-imposed silent retreat, where I stopped recognizing the sound of my own voice. I have a terrible sense of direction and am only fluent in English; what if I got lost and couldn't communicate with anyone to find my way? Also, I couldn't imagine eating meals, especially dinner, by myself. What was I supposed to do while I waited for the food to arrive? Wouldn't everyone around me think I was lame? And let's not forget that I am a small woman; wouldn't it be dangerous for me to be alone? I could be robbed or beaten or murdered. My brain spun with catastrophic scenarios that would put *Dateline* to shame.

When I was backpacking through Spain in college, traveling in a pack, we met another backpacker traveling solo and I remember thinking she must be weird or mean. Literally. I assumed she was traveling alone because no one was willing to travel with her, so she must have been either really weird or a real jerk. It was inconceivable to me that a reasonable woman would actually choose to travel by herself.

When my travel pack spent some time with her, it turned out that she was, shockingly, neither weird nor mean. She told us she was tired of following her friends' schedules and interests when they traveled together, so she decided to travel alone. I couldn't understand this at all; I concluded that, despite not being weird or mean, she was 100 percent crazy. Back then, if the choice was between traveling with convicted felons on parole or traveling alone, I would have chosen the felons. At least I would have known what I was getting into.

But now I faced a similar quandary. I could either wait forever for my friends' schedules and travel interests to match my own, or I could venture off by myself. Somehow, I chose the latter. I'm still not entirely sure how I got myself over the hurdle, but I think some combination of wine, a really expensive nonrefundable flight, and fear motivated me. I knew how bitter and angry I was feeling, and I also knew I didn't want those feelings to define me. I've always believed in the transformative power of travel, that it uniquely allows you to see yourself in a new way, out of your typical context—a travel consciousness, as it were. I couldn't think of any other way to prove to myself that I was charting a new and healthier course than to literally hit the road.

I decided that my first solo trip would be to Amsterdam, a city at the top of my must-see list. Since I was really worried about my safety and sanity alone in a foreign country, I did an absurd amount of research about every aspect of the trip and built a correspondingly absurd Excel spreadsheet to track my research. First, I researched the best and safest neighborhoods in Amsterdam. Once I narrowed down that list, I researched hotels in my selected postal codes and created a tab in my spreadsheet detailing the following factors:

- Central location: I wanted to be able to easily walk to get food and see the sites. The closer everything was to the hotel, the less likely I was to get lost or starve.

- Cost: I'm not a banker anymore, so I can't roll like one.

- Aesthetic: I thought I'd be happier in a place that aligned with my preferred visual aesthetic. Even I can't believe I was this anal-retentive. Seriously, there is a column in a spreadsheet labeled "aesthetic," and those cells are populated with comments like, "modern," "neo-classical," "Scandinavian," etc. Crazy, I know. "Neo-classical" won, but I am still not sure this was technically the correct description of the property.

- Views: it was Amsterdam after all, and I wanted to see a canal!

- Star Rating: presumably, a four- or five-star hotel would be more concerned than a lesser establishment about media coverage and reviews. Therefore, I reasoned, they would be more focused on ensuring that single guests were not routinely attacked or murdered. Fancy hotels should fundamentally be safer than less fancy ones. The challenge is that this factor conflicts with the aforementioned "I can't roll like a banker" criterion, resulting in a new table in my excel spreadsheet for cost tradeoff analyses.

- Trip Advisor ratings: I mean, real people don't lie on the internet. Right?

I also researched transit to and from the airport and around the city. I bought, and read fully, several guidebooks. This was basically obsessive-compulsive-disorder-style travel planning at its finest.

At the time, a good friend of mine lived in Hamburg, Germany, and she suggested that I visit her at the end of my trip. It made me feel safer to have planned friend time at the end of the trip to stem the vast loneliness I assumed I'd surely be experiencing by then, but Hamburg is actually pretty far away from Amsterdam. I decided to add an interim visit to Berlin to my itinerary. I love history (if only my ex-husband had been a history professor!), and Berlin obviously is rich with historical intrigue. I got so caught up in the planning that I didn't realize how ambitious my trip to Amsterdam— now, Amsterdam, Berlin, and Hamburg—had become. With so many details—hotels, activities, buses, trains, etc.—I had stopped focusing on the terror I was feeling about traveling solo. My spreadsheet had grown to four tabs, one for each city I was visiting, including hotel evaluations and selection, train timetables, potential daily itineraries, and all associated costs for each city; plus, one tab that provided a color-coded view of the entire ten-day trip. Every time a surge of panic would threaten, I would take comfort in my spreadsheet and find a new trip-planning activity to distract me. For example, I clearly needed to buy a new wardrobe for this trip.

On one unnecessary shopping trip, I spotted a lovely lime green sundress that just spoke to me (figuratively; despite the evidence to the contrary, I hadn't completely lost my mind). At the time, I didn't really wear a lot of dresses and certainly not lime green ones, so this was really unusual. My entire wardrobe reflected my mood of late and consisted of very boring, almost entirely black clothes—what I liked to call "work pants" and other boring basics. I definitely didn't own a fun green sundress. Statistically speaking, I didn't think I'd need it given my research on the typical May weather in Amsterdam and central/northern Germany, which was cool, cloudy, and rainy. But it was on sale, and I felt strangely compelled to buy it.

Shopping completed, my spreadsheet and I anxiously awaited departure day. When it arrived, I had a full-fledged panic attack, complete with the pounding heart and jelly legs that WebMD would surely tell me meant I was about to die. Luckily, I concluded I needed to call my therapist, not 911. After she talked me off the ledge, I solemnly headed to the airport, determined but absolutely terrified. My excitement for the trip was nonexistent; this was now all about surviving.

My flight was uneventful, as the best flights usually are. I stayed awake the whole time, innumerable cups of coffee fueling the re-reading of my Amsterdam and Germany guidebook collection. Upon landing, I nervously worked my way through customs and found the bus to the city center. I had no trouble finding my hotel, likely because I had visually committed its location to memory while trying to classify its architectural style. And I loved it! Neo-classical or not, the aesthetic was just right for me, and I could even see a small canal from my room! The breakfast room looked directly out onto one of the main canals. It was literally charm personified. Everything was going smoothly; nearly a full day of travel, and I hadn't gotten lost or murdered. Success!

Adding to my delight, it was a surprisingly sunny and warm day, so I decided to take a walk. Of course, I carefully mapped the route to my destination—the famous Amsterdam Flower Market, the only floating flower market in the world. And since it was so sunny and warm, it seemed like the perfect day to wear my new lime green sundress. And so it was that my pretty lime green sundress and I headed out of my hotel to explore the city. I found the city surprisingly walkable and easy to navigate (it's possible I had also memorized the entire map after months of research) and quickly strolled the short distance to the market. I was kind of amazed when I got there. I was so convinced that everything was going to be so hard on my own, and it just wasn't. Not only that, but it was beautiful!

And that's when it happened—a moment I will never forget, *that moment in Amsterdam.* Strolling alongside a charming canal, thousands of beautiful flowers in every color of the rainbow to my right, in shops atop houseboats docked along the water as other boats sailed by, feeling the warmth of the sun on my face as I meandered along the cobblestone walkways. I felt pretty and vibrant and fully alive, like I hadn't felt in years. And I realized why. I was exactly, precisely where I wanted to be, doing exactly what I wanted to do, and I had made that all happen through my own efforts. My obsessive research helped me choose my destination, my willingness to take a leap had gotten me here physically, and no grand benefactor was funding the travel. I felt empowered. Independent. Free. It was like a simultaneous flashback to the old adventurous, pre-marriage me, and a flash forward to the new me I could be if I only trusted myself enough to try. What else might I rediscover if I let the real me out again?

The rest of the trip really drove home this message of empowerment. While I had never believed I could or would want to travel alone, I actually learned of the many, many benefits. I had real, uninterrupted time to think and clear my head without the distractions of home. I didn't have to fill empty space with lame conversations, but I also had the opportunity to meet interesting people. As a solo traveler, you are free to talk or not to talk with whomever you'd like. People are more likely to approach you precisely because you are alone. I had thought this would be scary, but I realized it's quite easy to determine if someone is approaching you with good or bad intent. And meeting local people creates much deeper cultural understanding than just following a guidebook.

The ability to do whatever I wanted, whenever I wanted, was absolutely liberating. I realized I could change my plans at any time because I was the only one in charge. For example, when I found myself fascinated by the Checkpoint Charlie Museum in Berlin, I changed my plans and spent the full day there. For World War II history buffs, this place is just mind-blowing.

Traveling by myself also increased my ability to problem-solve, which in turn has driven increased resilience. When an announcement was made in German and everyone on my train to Hamburg started to get off, I had no idea what was going on and couldn't find anyone who spoke English to explain it to me. Finally, I found a businessman who spoke English, and he told me the train was terminating unexpectedly, so I would need to catch a new one. He also explained that there weren't a lot of English speakers in this rural part of Germany, so I should look for people in "business attire" if I needed any further help since most business is conducted in English. This, of course, was useful information. And successfully getting myself on the correct train with such well-dressed assistance made me feel super confident.

Of course, the trip wasn't perfect. The first few meals alone in Amsterdam were awkward; asking for a table for one and then sitting there, trying to figure out where to look and what to do while not eating, took some getting used to. And then there was that sketchy German guy who hit on me in a bar in Berlin and made me so uncomfortable that I left much earlier than I wanted to because I felt like he had bad intent. There was that confusing train issue, and also, a strangely traumatizing, life-size Genghis Khan plus horse statue in the hallway outside my hotel room in Berlin that I kept thinking was a real man with bizarre taste in hats trying to attack me. Seriously, every time I opened my door, I flinched. It did make it easier to find my room, I guess.

I came back home from Amsterdam a changed person, or maybe more of a restored person, really. Traveling so far out of my comfort zone both literally and metaphorically reminded me that I was independent and capable and could take care of myself. I could feel the transformative power of travel helping me to see myself objectively, slowly erasing my bitter edges. My situation at home was still the same, but my perspective was not. I realized I had choices.

Switzerland via Snowplow

I hate New Year's Eve. It is officially my least favorite "holiday" of the year. There is no good way to celebrate it, especially as a single person, although I didn't really like it when I wasn't single, either. I feel obligated to go out, even if I don't actually want to, because I cannot avoid the pitying looks I'll receive if I say I'm spending the evening alone. I would argue that "with my cat" is not alone, but my partnered friends seem to disagree. And, when I do go out, things are overcrowded and overpriced. But my biggest issue with New Year's Eve is the enormous weight of high expectations. It has to be the biggest, bestest, most exciting night of the year. And if one more person asks me who I'm going to kiss when the clock strikes midnight, I may just vomit.

That said, I don't like hating things. As an eternal optimist, I believe there must be a way to make all bad situations better, even extremely stupid, expectation-laden fake holidays. For this reason, I have engaged in a lifelong quest to find the best way to celebrate New Year's Eve. So far, my best New Year's Eve was the one where I bailed on a boring party to hang out at home with my cat, Chapstick, a beautiful glass of California cabernet, and Greek takeout.

A few years ago, it occurred to me that I should travel somewhere exciting for New Year's Eve. I love to travel; I hate New Year's. Perhaps the love for the former would offset the hatred for the latter. I shared this idea with a friend whose family, as it turned out, had a ski house in Switzerland; did I want to join her and her family this year for a New Year's ski trip? Apparently struck by a bout of temporary amnesia during which I forgot that I am a very, very crappy skier, I agreed. Skiing in Switzerland sounded like an awesome way to ring in the New Year and a glorious answer to probing questions about my "holiday" plans.

I booked my flights to Zurich and tried not to be overly self-congratulatory when addressing well-intentioned inquiries from condescending partnered friends about my "holiday" plans. Although it was super entertaining to watch their facial expressions evolve over the course of that conversation—from pity (clearly the single girl has no/lame plans) to surprise (wait, she has plans and they don't involve her cat?) to envy (I wish I was going to my friend's ski house in Switzerland!).

The night before I was scheduled to fly to Zurich, the weather forecast was ominous. A blizzard was about to hit New York. Undeterred, I headed to JFK International Airport early, convinced nothing would prevent me from getting to Switzerland. On the way to the airport, it was snowing insanely hard and the roads were slick. I arrived late and rushed to the ticket counter for the latest news. It was jammed with stressed-out people whose flights had all been canceled. I was still optimistic; I was going to succeed at my quest to have a great New Year's Eve. I waited in line to talk to the ticketing agent, who informed me that my flight to Zurich was indeed canceled and the next available direct flight was in three days, which was on New Year's Eve. Not ready to accept defeat, I asked if there were any other options to get me to Zurich sooner.

"Well, if you can get yourself to Newark Airport, I can put you on a flight connecting through Stockholm to Zurich."

Cheerfully, I agreed and she rebooked me on this new flight from Newark. Ticket confirmation in hand, I stepped away from the ticket counter.

And then it occurred to me: I was in Queens, New York, in the middle of a debilitating blizzard that had pretty much closed JFK Airport. Newark Airport is in New Jersey. How on earth was I going to get to Newark from Queens in the middle of a blizzard to catch my new flight? I called my parents for advice.

So, I love my parents, but this was not a good use of my phone-a-friend option. They are not huge travelers and are not fans of adventure. They got their passports at the same time I did, when I announced that I was going to study abroad in London, and they decided they were not sending their then nineteen-year-old youngest daughter on a flight across the Atlantic by herself. Their advice was clear: You cannot get to Newark. Find a hotel, wait out the storm, come back to their house in Connecticut once it was safe to travel again, and spend New Year's Eve at home with them.

I think that was what got me. No matter how much you love your parents, you absolutely cannot spend New Year's Eve at home with them as a divorced single woman without incurring the pity of the entire Universe. I was now determined to make my way to Newark and to Switzerland through Stockholm. So, I quickly got off the phone, assuring my parents I'd be in touch once I figured out my plans. They definitely thought that meant local hotel plans; I meant I'd let them know once I made my way to Newark.

So, now what? I was stranded at JFK, time was ticking away, and I needed to get to Newark. I walked toward the windows to think and formulate a plan. In the midst of my reverie, I realized that an older couple was standing a few feet from me. The man was wearing a puffy Dartmouth jacket. I also went to Dartmouth, so I took this as a sign. Like most Dartmouth alums, I have this deeply rooted notion that all Dartmouth alums around the (girdled) Earth are upstanding people and my long-lost best friends. It's totally normal for two alums who are complete strangers to act like best friends upon meeting and realizing they both have the granite of New Hampshire in their muscles and their brains. (Sorry, couldn't help myself; that's a line from the alma mater.) But seriously, all Dartmouth alums suffer from this bizarre affliction. I don't feel like that happens at most other schools, but then, I wouldn't know. So, I decided to approach the Dartmouth-jacket-wearing man. I introduced myself as we all do, stating name and graduating year. He did the same; as expected, we were now officially best friends.

Turns out that the Dartmouth guy and his wife were in a similar situation; their only chance of getting to Europe was to get to Newark that afternoon. I explained what I had figured out so far. The subway was running below ground during the storm. If we could get to a subway line, we could make our way to Penn Station and catch a train to Newark. The problem was that I couldn't figure out how to get to an open subway station in the middle of the blizzard. The roads were impassible and no taxis or cars were available. Staring out the window, we all pondered the fifteen plus inches of snow outside. There were definitely no taxis, just a few snowplows working feverishly to keep the snow at bay.

Suddenly, my new Dartmouth best friend exclaimed, "I've got it! We'll hire a snowplow to take us to the subway station!"

"We'll hire a snowplow? I'm not following," I said, beginning to question this man's sanity.

"Nothing can drive through this snow, but a snowplow can! Maybe if we pay one of these guys enough, he'll take us to the subway!"

Dartmouth Best Friend Guy was super excited about this plan. I was less excited, but I didn't have any better ideas, so I decided to go with it. Why not, right?

"All right, I'm in!" I was trying to feign excitement; I think it worked.

The three of us headed confidently to the nearest snowplow. This was not an "official" New York City snowplow. This was literally one of those beaten up big white vans with a snowplow attached to the front. You know, it's the kind of van Jeff Rossen from the *Today Show* is always warning you not to park next to in mall parking lots because crazy people with knives will jump out of them and try to rob or kidnap you. So, here I was with two complete strangers, approaching a big white van with a snowplow attached to ask for a ride to a subway station. Sounds smart.

Dartmouth Best Friend Guy made crazy crossing motions with his arms to call the attention of the snowplow driver. It was sort of a cross between the international "I'm choking" gesture and the motion air traffic controllers make when they are directing planes on the runway. It worked. The snowplow driver stopped and rolled down his window.

"Are you guys okay?" he asked.

"We're stuck here at the airport and we need a ride to a subway station. Can you take us?" said Dartmouth Best Friend Guy. I did my best to look not terrified and also reasonable, given that this request was kind of insane.

Snowplow Driver Guy looked puzzled. "Um, I'm working right now; I'm plowing out the airport. But maybe I can take you when I'm done working?" Snowplow Driver Guy was looking at us like we were crazy. He wasn't wrong.

"Right, but you see we're stuck and we need to get to Newark now. You're our only hope," said Dartmouth Best Friend Guy. I was starting to wonder if my new best friend was a politician. He was convincing. You could see the snowplow driver was hesitating.

"We'll pay you," continued Dartmouth Best Friend Guy. "We are going to miss our trips without your help. Please, sir, can you help us?"

Snowplow Driver Guy got out of the van and opened the back door. "All right, hop in," he said. Snowplow Driver Guy was a very large man. He had crates of strange-looking tools in the back of his van. We had not agreed to a price for this ride to the subway station. Dartmouth Best Friend Guy grabbed his and his wife's luggage, tossed the luggage and his wife in the van, jumping in after her, and waited for me to hop in. He seemed really excited. I was freaking out. Was I about to be murdered in a van in Queens with my new best friend and his wife? New Year's Eve with my parents was sounding better and better to me. Tossing my paranoia to the side, I said a silent prayer, put my luggage in the back of the van, and stepped in after it.

And then we were off to the subway station. Dartmouth Best Friend Guy seemed invigorated that a solution had been found. He and his wife discussed their travel plans excitedly. Meanwhile, I was hugging my purse as though it were a life jacket and I was on the verge of drowning, rocking back and forth in some sort of strange effort to keep calm. I was perched on the edge of my seat, eyeing the snowplow driver to see if he did anything suspicious. I was also furtively looking at the door locks, poised to make a quick escape should this go horribly wrong. Basically, I looked like a lunatic, or maybe more like an escaped convict fearing discovery.

After the longest fifteen minutes of my life, we arrived at a subway station. Snowplow Driver Guy hopped out of the van to open the back door for us.

"Man, we got here quick! The new vans couldn't do this! This van is tough, man. It can get through anything. They don't make 'em like they used to," he said as he looked affectionately at his van and helped us with our luggage. "Hope you guys make your flight." He offered his arm to help us out of his van.

That's right; the very large snowplow driver turned out to be a really nice guy who helped us with our luggage and made sure we got out of his van safely when he dropped us off at the subway station. We tried to pay him, but he refused, saying something about it being Christmas season, how great old vans are, and how he was happy he didn't buy a new one since this old one was so great. "They don't make 'em like they used to!"

Faith in humanity restored, I thanked him profusely and slipped twenty dollars into his hand. I think Dartmouth Best Friend Guy did the same.

From there, my new friends and I caught the subway to Penn Station. Settled on the train to Newark, it was time to call home and check in with my parents. My dad answered.

"Hey, Sara! We were wondering what hotel you ended up at!"

"Great news, actually! I'm on the train to Newark and I think there's a good chance I'll make my flight!"

"Really?" Dad sounded confused. "How did you manage that?"

"Well, I met a really nice Dartmouth guy and his wife who were in the same situation as me. We convinced a snowplow driver to take us to the subway station and then we took the subway to Penn Station, and now, I'm on the train to Newark."

There was a long pause while my father processed this.

"How did you all fit in the snowplow? There's no room for three people and luggage in a city snowplow."

"Well, it wasn't a city snowplow. It was one of those big white vans with the snowplow attached to the front."

"You got in the back of one of those big white vans???" Clearly, my father has watched the same Jeff Rossen reports that I have. "If I am understanding this correctly, you and two strangers hitchhiked on a for-hire snowplow in New York City in the middle of a blizzard. Have you lost your mind?"

I didn't really have a good response to this question beyond pointing out that I was alive and well and going to Switzerland.

The rest of this trip was far less eventful than its beginning. The flight from Newark was close to on time. I'm no expert in geography, but I learned that Stockholm and Zurich are much farther apart than I had previously realized. With all the drama, I arrived almost fifteen hours later than I was supposed to, but I made it and that's what counts.

Also, the temporary amnesia regarding my skiing ability most definitely faded in the Swiss Alps. I managed to somehow veer off the easy level run I was skiing and onto a run I was absolutely incapable of handling. I ended up stranded in the middle of this run, still wearing one ski, which was situated on *top* of the snow. My other, ski-less foot was stuck up to my knee *in* the snow. My ski was several feet away, and I couldn't extricate myself from my predicament to fetch it. Stuck literally in the middle of a ski run in Switzerland with my legs at an awkward ninety-degree angle, watching people who actually knew how to ski sail by me while I had no ability to move at all, I really had the opportunity to contemplate my choices over the past week and my feelings about New Year's Eve. Luckily, a very amused ski patrol person finally rescued me from my snow-prison and my thoughts.

This slightly hare-brained adventure to Switzerland was certainly proof of my reclaimed determination to clobber the obstacles in my path—not to mention the unexpected depth of support of the Dartmouth alumni community. Also, it really is the journey that counts, not the destination. That said, my best New Year's Eve so far was the one where I bailed on a boring party to hang out at home with my cat, Chapstick, a beautiful glass of California cabernet, and Greek takeout.

My Heart Belongs
to Santorini

———

S ingle or partnered, I have always considered myself a romantic. I am a Hallmark Channel super fan, owner of an embarrassingly extensive collection of romance novels, and a true believer in the power of love to inspire, delight, and make us better people.

So, it's a bit strange that the greatest love of my life is not a person, or even a pet, but an island halfway around the world—Santorini.

The first time I visited Santorini, I was in a terrible mental state. I had just finalized my long, contentious divorce and was trying to sell the house my husband and I had shared with the "help" of one of the world's worst realtors. The internal stresses were showing on the outside and I had packed on over forty pounds.

On top of this, I arrived in Santorini after attending my first post-breakup wedding. And the day before I left to attend that wedding, I received my divorce decree in the mail. When I opened the nondescript white envelope from the city of

Pittsburgh, it contained just one document bearing a large gold seal indicating that it was an original. It looked suspiciously like one of those award certificates I got in elementary school for being the best speller. Unclear if I was a spelling bee champion or a divorcee, I filed the letter and tried not to infer anything from the unfortunate timing of receiving one's divorce decree while preparing to travel to a wedding.

On the plus side, the wedding I attended was in Cyprus, a culturally Greek island country in the eastern Mediterranean, and the home of one of my closest friends. Aside from the groom and his immediate family, I was the only American to make the trip. In general, it seemed that few Americans made it all the way out there, so I felt a bit like a local celebrity. As soon as I opened my mouth on this British-English-speaking island, my American accent attracted an immediate, friendly following—a welcome distraction.

Even without the fanfare, Cyprus is fascinating. The island is known as the birthplace of Aphrodite, the Greek goddess of love, so I was expecting the many picturesque beaches and iconic Greek temple ruins. What I didn't realize was that the capital city, Nicosia, is the only divided capital in Europe; Turkey occupies the northern portion of the island, and a militarized border divides the city. Observing the challenges and tensions firsthand was a startling reality check in the midst of paradise and also an ironic reflection of my conflicted state of mind. It was amazing to celebrate love with dear friends in a stunning place but painful to be constantly reminded that love doesn't always work out as planned.

Although the wedding was beautiful—and exactly what I imagined a real *Big Fat Greek Wedding* on an actual Greek island to be—I was an emotional mess. I was intensely happy for my friends and intensely sad about the life I had lost. And sitting with such extreme emotions was excruciating. I felt keenly aware of how numb I'd become to avoid these feelings, and that made me feel even worse.

So, I left Cyprus for Santorini with a heavy heart and filled with cynicism. This was a strange experience for me because "cynical" was never a word anyone used to describe me before my divorce or even today. In fact, a former employee once described me as having two moods: sunny and less sunny. But in that moment, on a high-speed ferry sailing across the Aegean Sea for Santorini, when I should have been thrilled about the journey ahead, all I could feel was mistrust, and all I could see was what could go wrong.

Santorini had always been a dream destination. Pictures of the island held a sort of magnetic attraction for me and the power to stop me in my tracks. Whenever I would look through a European guidebook or travel brochure, my eyes always found Santorini. The beautiful white houses with blue domed roofs, the sheer drop of the cliffs, the navy-blue water—it seemed impossible to me that any place could really look like that. I knew I needed to see it in person.

And in my toxic mental state, I needed this impossible to be possible, but I was tortured by the fear of being disappointed again. I don't think I fully appreciated it at the time, but this trip was more than just an X on a bucket list; my world view lay in the balance. I'm not sure I could have handled another disappointment. I needed Santorini to be as beautiful as those pictures; I needed one dream to be real.

In the mad rush to get off the ferry and not crush anyone with my luggage, I didn't observe much as we sailed into the port. The ferry port itself wasn't remarkable, and I was primarily focused on getting out of there and away from the throngs of sweaty, not-respectful-of-American-standards-for-personal-space tourists as fast as possible. The bus was so crowded I couldn't see the view out of the windows. When I arrived at the main bus station, my mission was to find my hotel and wrangle my luggage up the uneven, crowded sidewalks.

A sweaty, bruised, pudgy mess, I finally found my hotel, one of the biggest in the capital city, Fira, high above the cliffs. The nice, English-speaking receptionist showed me to my room, a very simple and minimally furnished room facing the water. I recall feeling underwhelmed and slightly on the verge of panic.

And then she opened the doors to the balcony.

Everything in my world changed in that moment. I still feel shivers up and down my body when I think about it. It was the most beautiful view I had ever seen or imagined in my entire life. Hands down. Ever. The pictures I had spent years admiring could not even remotely capture what I saw in front of me. I was in awe in a way I had never experienced or believed was possible to experience. I was dumbfounded, speechless, overwhelmed, enchanted. I could not believe my eyes. I was in love.

I don't remember anything the hotel receptionist said to me after she opened those doors. I know at some point she left me alone, and I sat on my balcony for hours. Eventually, I grabbed my first-ever travel journal, which I had bought on a whim just a few days before, and wrote incoherently for several more hours, struggling to find words that could even come close to capturing the beauty in front of me.

Nowadays, I often find that writing helps me process my thoughts and emotions, and it can take a while to get to the good stuff. But at that time, writing on purpose was still a totally foreign act; I wasn't even sure why I'd felt compelled to buy a travel journal in the first place. And then I saw that view and was so overwhelmed with emotions, I needed a way to get them out. Strangely, writing was the only solution that came to mind. And once I started, I couldn't seem to stop. Something about Santorini created a visceral need to express myself that I had never felt before.

After pages of failed attempts at defining beauty, I discovered these words on the page in front of me:

> *I feel like my ability to truly marvel at the world has returned. I also didn't realize I had lost my ability to marvel at the world until I wrote that last sentence. I think Santorini is bringing back my lost sense of wonder; I can't think of anything I've marveled at in the recent past. Can a place bring you back to a part of yourself that you've lost?*

In that moment, seeing the most beautiful thing I had ever seen in my life, my sense of wonder returned. Funny thing was, I hadn't realized it was missing, and how much I missed having it around. It was like that feeling of getting new glasses and realizing how bad your vision was before. Everything seemed clear, crisp, and new. Suddenly, I remembered what possibility felt like; that there are things so amazing and beautiful that the only appropriate response is awe. It was as if my eyes had been reopened to the world after an unintentionally long sleep, or maybe, a self-induced coma.

Santorini was created about 3,500 years ago when a relatively large, round, volcanic island exploded, leaving just the edges of the circle around a huge flooded volcanic crater, called the caldera. The island is shaped like a backward letter "C," and the capital city of Fira sits on the edge of the crater in the center of the "C." From the perspective of Fira—and this is an island where perspective matters—I could see the full caldera, the famously picturesque city of Oia to my right at the top of the "C," glimmering white above the black rocks, and the Faros lighthouse to my left at the bottom of the "C." Across from me, the island of Thirassia looked like a giant alligator perched on the sea, its face pointing south, its tail pointing north and a white stripe of houses along its back. Two flat, black volcanic islands with irregular ink blot edges seemed to ooze like baking cookies ever closer toward the main island, next to a tiny white island that looked like a tiramisu. And of course, the navy-blue waters of the caldera, the flooded volcanic crater, filled the gaps between the land and the sea.

The most dramatic part was the scale of the crater's cliffs. The caldera's edge is not a gentle slope easing into the Aegean. Instead, bright white and blue buildings cling to the cliffs' edges, dangling hundreds of feet above the sea. It's as if a cubist painting sprang from its canvas and landed gracefully, if precariously, along the cliff's edge. Mazes of staircases swirl everywhere, up and down with no apparent pattern. Doorway arches mark entrances to more staircases to who knows where. Balconies protrude out at bizarre, unnatural, structurally impossible angles. People and donkeys wander the streets as the sun sparkles off the water and casts dramatic shadows between buildings. It is a study in contrasts, order in the chaos.

I spent the next several days romping around Santorini like a child, except one with a credit card and of legal drinking age.

I've always had this philosophy that I would never visit the same place twice by choice. With so many places to see and so little time, it seemed inefficient. But that all changed in Santorini. I felt a visceral need to return as soon as possible. I changed some plans and somehow got myself back there two months later in the most circuitous way possible: Pittsburgh to Philly to Frankfurt to Athens to Santorini. I was *that* determined to get back.

Part of me expected to find it less astounding than I had on the first visit. The inner cynic that had been with me for so long wasn't going down without a fight. But the second I opened my balcony door and took in that awe-inspiring view under the warmth of the Aegean sun, it was clear that the battle was over and my sense of wonder had won. I couldn't unsee the physical beauty around me and I couldn't un-feel the joy I felt. I knew I'd be back as often as I could, if only to experience that feeling that was absent from my everyday life for way too long.

The following summer, I decided to take a longer trip to Santorini. In the year between visits, a lot had changed. I had finally moved out of the house I'd shared with my husband and into an apartment I loved. I'd lost the forty post-divorce pounds and started taking a Greek language class at a local Greek Orthodox church. In many ways, Santorini inspired me to make these changes. I was able to see the possibilities more clearly than I had in years, and that made changing less scary.

This trip, I stayed in a different hotel in Santorini—a family-run bed-and-breakfast, known for amazing food to rival the amazing views. When I arrived in the marble lobby, down a short flight of stairs from the winding road above, I saw three people crowded behind the check-in counter. The younger man introduced himself in perfect English.

"You must be Sara, from America. I am Dimitris, but you can call me Jim if you prefer."

"Jim? Why would I call you Jim if your name is Dimitris?" I said this in Greek, or at least, I tried to.

"Are you Greek?" asked the woman in Greek. To Dimitris, she said, "Why didn't you tell me she's Greek?" To me, she asked in Greek, "Are you hungry? What would you like to eat?"

"Well, I'm American, but my family is Italian."

"Why are you speaking in Greek if you are American and Italian?" asked Dimitris.

"*Una faccia, una razza!*" the woman exclaimed, in Italian. "What would you like to eat?" she asked, again in Greek.

Now the older man jumped in.

"I am Elias, this is my wife, Lyra, and this is our hotel!" He was speaking in English. "Italians and Greeks are the same, we think, so we have the expression, '*una faccia, una razza*'—'one face, one race.' So, you are Greek like us. And please, tell Lyra what you would like to eat or she will cook the whole kitchen."

I loved these people immediately. By virtue of being Italian, I was Greek and also, adopted. I later learned that Dimitris is exactly my age, and his parents are the same ages as my actual parents. It was like I stepped into an alternate universe, complete with a family.

Lest Lyra cook the whole kitchen and given my incredibly limited tourist Greek vocabulary, I told her that I love Greek desserts. She ran through a list of her favorites and mentioned *pasta flora,* a delicious pastry with apricot jam. I told her that this was one of my favorites, too, and she hugged me. I loved this family.

Dimitris, who I refused to call Jim, showed me to my beautiful room with a giant balcony and jaw-dropping views.

"It's huge!" I exclaimed when we entered the room. I wasn't expecting the room and balcony to be so big. It actually looked smaller in the pictures online.

"Would you like me to find you a smaller one?" he asked, clearly joking. We embraced a brother-sister vibe from the start.

I took a walk to reacquaint myself with beautiful Santorini. I walked for hours around the winding streets, trying to figure out how the pathways, stairs, and doorways connected. I lost track of time, mesmerized by this strange place where doorways sometimes opened onto stairs, sometimes opened onto houses, and sometimes seemed to open to nothing at all. All the doorways felt like a metaphor that I couldn't quite construct in my brain, but I kept trying to find it. It made taking a walk feel like a choose your own adventure novel.

And this may be accurate, given that my phone claimed that I climbed sixty-seven flights of stairs. After my long walk (climb), I came back to my room to find a freshly baked *pasta flora* with apricot jam, still warm from the oven, courtesy of Lyra. That night, I watched the most beautiful sunset in the world with a glass of crisp Santorini Assyrtiko, an amazing local white wine, and homemade *pasta flora*. It was divine.

At breakfast the next morning, I had the opportunity to thank my hosts for the delicious *pasta flora* and their kindness in making me feel so at home in their hotel. Lyra and I talked for hours and connected over Greek food, having a conversation probably about a third in Greek and the rest in English. She invited me to her kitchen so she could teach me how to make *galaktoboureko*, my favorite Greek pastry, which is layers of phyllo filled with lemon-semolina custard and topped with simple syrup. So, the next morning I found myself in the kitchen with Lyra, making *galaktoboureko*, like it was the most normal thing in the world for a random American and her newly adopted mom from halfway around the world to be cooking together.

Later that week, we went shopping for local tomatoes and she brought me to her home to see her farm. It felt as though I had been adopted, not just by my Greek mom, but by her whole family, and it feels like that every time I visit.

For the past decade, I have visited Santorini at least once a year, always staying with my adopted family. Over the years, I've enjoyed many home-cooked dinners, attended church services and yoga classes, met other family friends, and even joined family parties for name days—a Greek tradition where one celebrates the person who shares a name with a saint on that saint's celebration day. It really feels like I have another family in Santorini, which completely blows my mind.

On one visit to Santorini, I was hanging out with Dimitris, and he asked if I was interested in taking a sailboat tour of the caldera. His friend, a retired Greek Navy captain, had just started a new sailing company on the island, and Dimitris wanted to send some business his way. I love seeing Santorini from the water. It's a totally different experience to look up at the giant cliffs from below; it strangely magnifies the awe. But I don't know how to swim and am terrified of deep water, so I generally avoid boat tours. In Santorini, the boat tours find a place to anchor in the very deep caldera and allow time for the guests to jump into the water for a swim, which was the last thing I could imagine doing. So, I hesitated.

"I promise you will be safe with Captain John," Dimitris said. "He's an old family friend."

The next day, I was sitting in the sunshine at the southern harbor of Santorini, when one of the most beautiful men I have ever seen approached me. He looked to be in his mid-thirties and was tall with dark hair and deeply tanned olive skin, wearing crisp white sailing shorts and a baby-blue polo shirt.

"Are you Sara?" he asked in crisp English with a very elegant accent. He had a melodious and deep voice and sounded precise and confident. "I am Captain John."

I was floored. When Dimitris told me about his retired navy captain friend, I was thinking he would be a retiree—i.e., not a stunning man about the same age as me. This was going to be an interesting day.

I followed Captain John to his sailboat, a beautiful double-masted vessel. There I met the other tourists who would be joining me on this adventure: Rebecca, a young Australian businesswoman and mom with her precocious five-year-old son, Matt.

We immediately hit it off. Matt acted more like a retiree than Captain John. And Captain John regaled us with stories as we sailed, including a time when he narrowly avoided pirates off the coast of Africa. After a few hours, the boat dropped anchor. Rebecca and Matt jumped happily into the water. I, of course, did not.

"Why aren't you swimming?" asked John.

"I can't swim."

"You can't, or you don't want to?"

"I can't. I never learned."

"It's easy; I'll teach you!"

"No!" I practically shouted. "I don't like the water."

"You obviously like the water or you wouldn't come to Santorini every year." It's hard to explain how easily John seemed to understand how to deal with me.

"Okay, I'm afraid of the water."

"Well, that's different." Wrapping his large hands gently around my forearms, staring deeply into my eyes, John said, "You cannot visit Santorini and miss the experience of being in this water. I promise I will keep you safe. You must trust me."

How was I supposed to say no to this sweltering hot retired navy captain, who had protected his crew from *pirates* and was now staring into my eyes and promising to keep me safe?

And this is how I ended up, terrified, wearing a life vest, in the four-hundred-meter-deep Santorini caldera with Captain John by my side. And it was incredible.

As we sailed back to the harbor, Rebecca and I sat on the back of the sailboat with our feet in the water, wine glasses in hand, watching the sunset—what Rebecca called our "Jackie O. moment." It was the most perfect way to end a most unexpected and delightful day.

After that experience, John and I bonded and are still friends; we see each other every summer in Santorini. I am not sure if I believe in past lives, but I think if I do, I was married to John in one of them. We have an uncanny connection, an ability to really see each other that surprises me anew every time I see him. Once, I ended up at dinner with John and Lyra, and it was the funniest experience because it felt like I was having dinner with my partner and my mom, which wasn't true, but sort of was in a Santorinian alternate universe way.

Over the years and visits, I count many locals among my dearest friends—artists, yoga instructors, bartenders, tour guides. Every time I visit Santorini, it's a reunion of family and friends. Dimitris opened a rooftop bar recently that has become my Santorinian *Cheers*—a bar on the other side of the world where everyone knows my name. It blows my mind every visit.

Over a decade ago, my first visit to Santorini changed my life. I assumed it was because of the way the supernatural beauty and magic of the island instantly washed away a lifetime of cynicism and continued to recharge me every time I returned. I always say that Santorini is my happy place. But recently, I've realized it's become much more than that to me. It's become my safe place, the one place in the world where I can be the absolute best and truest version of myself, where I can go to clear my head and refresh, my spiritual home.

Every time I arrive in Santorini, whether by air or by sea, I am perched on the edge of my seat, waiting for that first glimpse of the island's dramatic cliffs. My heart beats faster. I feel the anticipation in my blood. What will I see this time? Who will I meet? What will I discover? And every time I leave, I feel heartbroken but also deeply grateful for the gift of time there. It's the perfect long-distance relationship, a partner who teaches without talking and always waits for me with open arms. Sometimes I'll close my eyes wherever I am in the world and see that perfect view, emblazoned in my memory, etched into the backs of my eyelids, and I'm instantly returned to that moment when childlike wonder replaced cynicism and I was changed forever.

Home is where your heart is, and my heart belongs to Santorini.

Bosses, Budgets, and Bikinis

———

My weight loss journey began by command of my brilliant and powerful boss. I was sitting in her office one day in my too-tight pants, complaining about how uncomfortable I was and how unhappy I felt with the way I looked. That morning, I had realized that my too-big thighs had actually worn a hole through the lining of my too-tight pants, so things were really at an all-time low.

I haven't historically had a healthy relationship with food. I love to eat, I have a sweet tooth (a mouth full of them), and I don't enjoy cooking—not exactly a recipe for dietary success. My husband was a good influence on me in the food department because he was willing to share cooking duties and strove for balanced meals. When he left, I defaulted to my baser instincts, processed sugar foods requiring minimal preparation. For a few months after the split, my weight and my diet were in some sort of equilibrium. I was so anxious all the time that I either wasn't eating or was burning off enough calories to offset my horrendous diet. Eventually and predictably, the balance shifted. I am actually not sure of the order of operations here—if I was feeling more comfortable on my own and gaining weight without the benefit of the anxiety-fueled metabolism, or if I was feeling more comfortable because the comfort foods I was eating were working their eponymous magic. Either way, I had packed on enough weight about a year after my relationship split to actually split my pants. Not good.

That said, I should have realized that complaining was never a good idea when talking to this particular boss. I've worked for many people in my life, across several different industries, but Veronica is my all-time favorite. Other colleagues seriously suggested that I create and run a fan club for her because my devotion ran that deep.

First of all, Veronica is a brilliant marketer. I am always happiest when I am learning something new, and I literally learned something new every day when I worked for her—the marketing things she planned to teach me, and other things I learned by observing the way she perfectly handled the craziest situations. Veronica was incredibly direct, so I always understood what she needed from me and why. She was the antithesis of a micro-manager, leaving me to work independently on my projects and trusting that I would reach out when necessary, and I loved her for every independent second she blessed me with.

Above all, she valued competence and a problem-solving mentality. Identifying a problem without potential ways to solve it was career suicide. Possibly as a result, she was a slightly terrifying figure to people who weren't willing to go the extra mile, didn't care as much as she did, or for any other reason, didn't meet her very high expectations. This widespread fear was a huge asset to me as her not fearful employee. When the team was uncooperative, all I had to say was, "I really don't think Veronica will be happy with this," and everyone would jump to do whatever I had just asked. It was awesome. I have never worked for anyone else who could make things happen just by the sheer power of her personality. Amazing.

So, anyway, Veronica was not a huge fan of complaints or complainers, and I was the adoring president of her fan club. I had also just presented a complaint without a corresponding potential solution. The company we worked for had a partnership with Weight Watchers and employees could attend on-site meetings each week without having to leave the office. Veronica suggested I join.

"Weight Watchers is like a budgeting system with food. You love budgets. This will be perfect for you!"

Despite the convenience of this potential solution, I was hesitant. I didn't think it was for me and wasn't interested in joining a "program." I've clearly watched too many *Dateline* episodes about people inadvertently joining cults.

That said, I do love budgets. It's a strange remnant from years working in finance; give me a budget to play with and an Excel spreadsheet and I'm as happy as a clam. It's like a money puzzle! Still, I was not convinced. I love to eat, especially foods of the decadent, carb-laden variety. A food budget limiting such decadence did not sound even slightly fun, but I was powerless to object. I had posed a problem without a solution; I had broken the cardinal rule. Minutes after voicing my complaint, Veronica had signed me up for the on-site Weight Watchers program. There was no backing out now without incurring the condemnation of one of the people I admired most, who was also my boss.

The next week, I reluctantly headed to my first meeting. To say I was not excited would be a supreme understatement. I was filled with dread. At this point, my diet consisted almost entirely of carbs, usually in the form of pasta and Twinkies, and caffeine, specifically Dunkin' coffee light and sweet—coffee with extra cream and extra sugar. In fact, my typical afternoon snack was an extra-large light and sweet coffee with two donuts. That was just a snack. I didn't even have to place my order when I walked into Dunkin'; the folks at my local shop knew me by name and my order by heart. I hadn't bought, prepared, or eaten a vegetable in years. I scoffed at fruit. This would not be an easy adjustment.

I entered the conference room where the meeting would be held and was greeted by a really peppy, thin, blonde lady and a scale. Of course she seemed happy; she was thin and didn't have to get on the scale. I felt a bit like Marie Antoinette as I stepped up to the scale; the peppy blonde lady was my executioner, and I really, really wanted some cake to ease the pain. Then I stepped on the scale and it was bad. Like all caps BAD. I had no idea how much weight I had gained, but that number certainly explained the pants situation. Wanting to cry and drown my sorrows with coffee and donuts, I dejectedly picked up my cult—sorry, program—materials and looked for a seat in the far corner of the room where I could pout more easily.

During the meeting, the peppy blonde lady welcomed us, a group of my seemingly equally dejected colleagues, all staring at the conference table with the downward gaze and slumped shoulders of post-weigh-in misery. Then she showed us her "before" picture and explained how the program worked. I was shell-shocked, horribly upset by how much weight I had gained, and felt like there was no way I was going to succeed. And oh, by the way, not only would I fail for myself, but I would also let Veronica down as well. Not awesome.

Eventually, I managed to direct my attention away from my defeatist inner dialogue to learn a bit about how the program worked:

- I had a daily points total that represented the total amount of food I could eat in a day.

- Every food had a points value. Anything I liked eating had a million points. Anything I didn't like eating had none.

- I was supposed to keep track of everything I ate and its points value every day so that it all added up to my daily points total. This part, at least, made sense to me, the "food budget."

When the meeting ended, I went back to my desk. It was 1:00 p.m.—time for my coffee break! Yay!

And then I realized I had to track my coffee break.

I whipped out my points calculator and came to the appalling realization that my regular snack would be my full day's worth of points. What was I supposed to do now? Angrily, I stormed out of the office to clear my head and figure out how to meet my caffeine needs in this new world. How could this "program" possibly work if I couldn't eat two donuts and drink a huge coffee full of extra cream and extra sugar every afternoon? I got to Dunkin' Donuts and meekly ordered a small coffee with cream and sugar, not extra of either. That was seven points. It was a sad moment for me. The folks at Dunkin' were confused and so was I. What had I gotten myself into?

That night, I got home from work and had no idea what I could eat. I assessed the situation and began to panic. My kitchen was stocked with pasta, frozen French fries, and instant mashed potato mix; dinner was typically some combination of the above, pizza, or a Chipotle burrito the size of my whole head. My freezer was filled with full-fat ice cream, a pint of which I believed also made a lovely dinner option. I also had every manner of processed cookie, brownie, or other pastry you can think of, including a club-size box of Twinkies. The club-size box of Twinkies enabled me to make the amazing "Twinkie-misu"—Twinkies soaked in coffee and Kahlua and then smothered in pudding to make a delicious, tiramisu-like delight. In retrospect, I have no idea how my blood hadn't caramelized with my all-sugar diet. The portions I could eat of these foods were miniscule; I needed options.

I went to the grocery store and, for the first time, actually walked around the produce section. I am not kidding; I had never bought fruits or veggies in the two years I had lived in that house. I was befuddled. It was like stepping into a foreign land of salad-eating healthy people. I was surrounded by foods I couldn't identify in their raw form. For example, I had never eaten a fresh cherry—I only ate things like cherry pie and black cherry ice cream—so I didn't realize fresh cherries came with pits. That wasn't a fun first bite. I bought the few things I could identify and went home, now completely certain I was going to fail.

That said, Veronica is pretty much always right. My love of budgets began to translate to this new food world. It became almost fun to figure out what I could eat every day. I began to understand important things like how many glasses of wine I could drink and still have points left for actual food. Wine has fewer points than beer, so I doubled down on my wine consumption. I discovered that fruits and veggies are not the devil. I also realized that getting pissed off at the number of points in an item I loved did not actually help the situation, and I reluctantly gave up both my anger and my Twinkies. And I learned that sugar rushes and the corresponding crashes I had always thought were normal were in fact quite avoidable. Shockingly, it felt good to not be at their whim.

And suddenly, I was actually losing weight. I'm not sure why this was such a surprise to me. I mean, that was the point, right? It's called *Weight* Watchers. But I was positively stunned at my next weigh-in to see that I was down six pounds! I don't think these results are typical, but they kind of made sense considering the complete 180-degree diet change from extraordinarily hideous to something closer to balanced. And then the weight continued to come off. Lower and lower, my weight dropped below even my goal weight, a number I had never thought was possible when I had set it in the first place. Suddenly, all of my clothes were literally falling off my body. I was in shock. I had to go shopping.

Shopping for clothes had always been a bipolar experience for me. I liked the idea of shopping—new things! Inspiration! But clothes never seemed to fit me the way they were supposed to. (Shoes are another story. Shoes love me no matter how much weight I gain.) I struggled to understand what styles would flatter my shape and the net result was crankiness replacing that initial shopping excitement nearly every time I stepped into a clothing store. It made me extremely unpleasant to shop with and extremely willing to compromise on suboptimal solutions to expedite the process.

Once I found an item that wasn't totally awful-looking, I would buy twelve of them. So, I had a closet full of twelve pairs of the same pants, twelve matching jackets because I thought suits were slimming, twelve knit tops in different colors—not a lot of style, not a lot of creativity. I chose basic clothes to hide myself in because the truth was that I never liked what was under them very much. But now, I really needed to shop. It was getting hard to be taken seriously at work when, with my clothes falling off, I looked alternately like a homeless person or a stripper with a terrible sense of style.

So, I went to my usual store and headed to the area I was used to going to—my old size clothes. I picked up a skirt maybe one or two sizes smaller than I used to wear and held it up to my waist. The woman working at the shop looked at me strangely.

"Do you need some help?" she asked.

"I'm trying to figure out if this is a good color for me."

"For you?" She was still looking at me strangely.

"Yes, for me," I answered, puzzled.

She looked at me like I was a complete moron. "That's not your size."

"It's not?"

She pursed her lips and raised her eyebrows, as if she thought I was completely insane. "No, that is way too big for you."

"Is it? That's so exciting! What size am I, do you suppose?"

Her pursed lips turned into a full scowl; I'm pretty sure she thought I was being a complete bitch when I was genuinely ecstatically happy.

"You don't know what size you are?" she said in a poorly disguised surly tone.

Now I became aware of our miscommunication.

"Look at me! I look ridiculous!" I said as I gestured to my baggy mess of an outfit. "I need new clothes because I just lost forty pounds and I don't have a clue what I'm doing." I realized I was literally out of breath. "I have no clothes!"

And then her expression softened and she became my new best friend. I felt like Anna Kendrick's character in *Pitch Perfect* when she realized that mean girls have issues, too.

"Oh honey, that's awesome! Let me help you!" She was now talking to me kind of the way I talk to my cat when he does something unexpectedly delightful, like scratching the scratching mat instead of me or my carpet.

We hooked arms (not really) as she led me across the store to the clothes six sizes smaller than when I first began this journey. Yep, *six* sizes. For several hours, I tried on pretty much everything in the store and bought pretty much everything I tried on. It was my *Pretty Woman* moment, minus the questionable career choices and rich guy paying the bill. This shopping spree continued in full force for a few years. Apparently, I was subconsciously trying to offset years of not-shopping with years of over-shopping to achieve some sort of shopping equilibrium. I was actually spontaneously offered a holiday-season job without actually applying at one of my favorite retailers. According to the store manager, "You're always here, you have all of our clothes, and you're so happy! If you worked here, you'd save so much money!"

I seriously considered it.

The other unexpected thing that happened with my weight loss was that I learned something new about human bodies: It is possible to be both thin and flabby at the same time. Having always been on the other side of pudgy, I wasn't aware that this was a possibility, but suddenly found myself in this strange middle ground. I finally understood why thin people exercised, a long-standing mystery solved. After many failed attempts at what seemed like every new exercise craze, I rediscovered yoga. It was the only form of exercise that required both my mental and physical focus; every time my mind would wander, I would fall on my face. The effort to keep my nose intact resulted in the calmest and fittest me I had ever been. Never an athletic person, I was surprised by how much stronger I was and by all the cool things my body could now do.

It really blows my mind when I stop to think about it all. I never thought I would succeed. I never believed I could be a thin, fit person, and it took a really long time to process this new me. For years, I looked in the mirror and was surprised to see myself. I had spent my entire life plagued by self-consciousness. I have pictures of myself on spring break in college wearing long shorts and a baggy T-shirt on the beach next to my bikini-clad friends. I had never owned a two-piece bathing suit; in fact, I had never learned to swim at least partly because I wanted to be as covered up as possible. Without all the extra weight, I started to feel unburdened—both physically and emotionally. I am still amazed at how freeing and empowering it is to be comfortable in your own skin.

I bought my first bikini and wore it in public on a ski trip with friends (in the hot tub, not while skiing; I'm not crazy). I briefly considered sending a picture to Veronica, who had moved on to a new company, but realized that would be really weird.

The Inadvertent Tupperware Party

———

B eing happily alone doesn't mean I'm always happy being alone. Sometimes things happen and I really wish I didn't have to deal with them by myself. Ironically, the fact that I have to figure these things out solo means that I do, which makes me increasingly less aggravated and more confident when other crazy things happen. A mouse taught me this lesson.

It was 4:00 a.m. and I woke up suddenly to a strange sound coming from downstairs. My eleven-year-old cat, Chapstick, who never missed a chance to sleep next to her human, was missing. I decided to investigate.

When I got to the bottom of the stairs, I was greeted by an unusual sight. Chapstick was frantically running around the dining room, super excited. This was not normal behavior for her. For the past several years, she was much more likely to sleep on her toys than play with them. I got closer. I noticed Chapstick had a toy in her mouth. Then I noticed the toy was moving—a live mouse. I watched in horror as Chapstick dropped the mouse, let it run around a bit, and then caught it again in her mouth. It was one of those moments when I really wished I was not living alone in the big house I would never have bought had my ex-husband not insisted—a house with mice, apparently. Clearly, this was not going to end well for the mouse, obviously, or for me, who would have this mouse's untimely death on my conscience while cleaning up his eviscerated remains from my lovely dining room carpet. Since it was 4:00 a.m., I couldn't call anyone. I had to figure this out on my own.

And then my other cat, Twinkie, appeared. Twinkie, a darling brown and grey tabby cat, was quite different from her petite older sister. Twinkie was the sweetest cat, if not the brightest, while Chapstick was a Napoleon-complex-laden genius. I am pretty sure Chapstick could have taken over the universe with the simple addition of opposable thumbs. However, Twinkie was a practiced mouser. The last time she had encountered a mouse, it had ended with a scene straight out of a horror movie. I had to act fast. I quickly grabbed Twinkie and tossed her, unsuspectingly, into the downstairs bathroom. As soon as the door closed, she realized she was missing out and started to wail-whine in that special way only cats can. But I had to stay focused on Chapstick and my mission to rescue the mouse.

How do you convince your genius cat to surrender her new favorite toy? This was the question my addled 4:00 a.m. brain attempted to answer. A solution appeared in my mind—Tupperware. I grabbed a Tupperware container from the kitchen cabinet and starting following Chapstick around the house on all fours, trying to entice her to drop the mouse. We did this for a while, as Twinkie continued to wail-whine/howl from the bathroom, and finally, success! Chapstick dropped the mouse; I caught him under the Tupperware! Great! Now what?

I decided to push the Tupperware container to the front door of my house, open it and shove container plus mouse out of the house and to safety. Genius! My house was one of those really long rectangular houses, and we were in the middle of the house when I caught the mouse. So, I army crawled to my front door, pushing the terrified mouse-in-Tupperware, who was doing mouse somersaults as we moved. Chapstick followed behind me, in full kitty pounce mode—low to the ground, making that hissing, chirpy hunting sound. Twinkie really knew she was missing out on some fun now; her wailing from the bathroom got even louder. Finally, I reached the front door! And then I realized that my old house had this weird raised wooden board that divided the entry area from the hallway. No way could I slide the Tupperware over this bump in the floor without releasing the mouse. I needed to revise my plan. So, I thought, back door!

And back through the whole first floor of the house we went, me on all fours, crawling, pushing the mouse-in-Tupperware, who was still doing somersaults, possibly more frantically. Chapstick was now very mad; her hissing and chirping sounds had elevated to full growls. She was following directly behind me, low to the ground, waiting for me to lose focus. Twinkie was now shrieking from the bathroom. I finally got to the back door. The floor was flat. I thought I would succeed. I awkwardly held down the mouse-in-Tupperware while unlocking the door. I quickly opened it and threw the mouse-in-Tupperware out the back door! He survived! I slammed the door shut to make sure Chapstick didn't run after him.

And then I remembered that I didn't shut the house alarm off. I remembered this because my house began shouting at me: "Burglary! Burglary! Exit immediately!" my house shouted at me. "Burglary!"

Chapstick was beyond furious. Twinkie was now making some weird cross between a meow and a shriek (shreow? meo-iek?). I don't know; it was loud. My phone started ringing. The house was shouting. I scrambled to grab the phone amidst the chaos.

"Ma'am, we have a report of an alarm being set off at your home. Are you okay? What is your password?" said the alarm company phone lady.

"My cat caught a mouse and I was chasing her to save the mouse and then the other cat tried to help her and I put her in the bathroom and got the mouse out of the house, but I forgot about the alarm and I think I am okay and the mouse is okay." Every possible horrible cat noise was also happening at this time.

"Ma'am, is there a burglar in your house?"

"No, there was a mouse, but I saved him."

"A mouse? I just need your password. We can't help you with rodents. What is all that noise?"

I somehow remembered the password and convinced the lady that I was not a crazed burglar but rather a regular single person with cats and a mouse problem doing what regular single cat people do when such problems emerge at 4:00 a.m. Finally, the house stopped shouting. I let Twinkie out of the bathroom; she suspiciously explored the whole first floor but decided she was ultimately more interested in sleeping. It was now 4:30 a.m. after all.

I'm pretty sure Chapstick never forgave me.

International Yoga

———

Rediscovering yoga after my divorce has kept me grounded and sane, which is saying a lot given how wound up I am by nature. I've learned many unexpected lessons from the practice, including how to manage a giggle fit in the most beautiful place in the world.

I first tried yoga early in my marriage. I really liked it and encouraged my husband to join me, but it wasn't his cup of tea. He preferred more aggressive forms of exercise, like kickboxing, which I generally hate. And for some reason, I had this idea that exercise was something we should do together. As a result, I enthusiastically signed up to try every high-intensity fitness fad while we were married, only to quit after a few weeks, leaving both of us frustrated and out of shape. I really don't know why it was so important to me that we exercise together that I was willing to forgo exercise entirely, but whatever. He left and I rediscovered yoga, so it all ended well.

An added benefit of yoga is that it is not a fad; it exists everywhere around the world. I completed my yoga instructor training a few years ago in Costa Rica. Yoga in the middle of a coffee plantation is the definition of balance. I practice as often as I can at home and try to keep it up when I travel. Imagine my delight when I discovered a new yoga studio at my favorite holiday spot—Santorini, Greece.

I excitedly made my way to the studio, which was no easy feat given the remote location in the center of the island, off the bus route. It was a pretty nondescript two-story building from the outside. When I walked in, I realized it was actually more like a giant square loft, with super high ceilings and tall windows draped with flowing white curtains. A staircase at the back corner of the space appeared to lead to a lofted bedroom above. I saw a bin with yoga mats but no obvious place to check in. Several other students arrived and set up their mats, but I wasn't sure what to do.

As I awkwardly considered my options, I noticed some activity on the stairs. Two absolutely stunning people had begun a graceful descent from the loft above. With regal posture and dressed head to toe in white, they appeared to be Greek Gods returning to earth from Mount Olympus. The man was tall, with dark hair and a golden, tanned complexion. He looked like that incredibly gorgeous model from the Acqua Di Gio cologne ads; he radiated confidence. The woman had golden blonde hair and was statuesque, almost like a Greek Charlize Theron. I stared at them in awe as they floated toward me. I was so caught off guard that my Greek words escaped me, and I blurted out something vaguely like, "Time for yoga!" in English in their general direction. In truth, there was no chance I would have been able to communicate with them in Greek, but I like to pretend that was a real option.

With a flourish of his white-clad arm, the stunning man announced dramatically, "I am Adonis. This is my wife, Electra." I was now fully gawking at the two most dazzling and appropriately named people I had ever encountered in my entire life. Had Electra been named Aphrodite, I might have literally died from perfection overload. Also, I realized that Adonis appeared to actually be wearing a white robe. His outfit had some serious cape action happening. Electra's robes seemed somehow humbler, like she was the more approachable God-like creature of the two. Somehow, I managed to communicate that I would like to take their sunset yoga class that evening, grabbed a mat and settled in for what was sure to be an interesting class. I took a moment before class began to lie on my back and reflect about how completely unbelievable it was to be in Greece celebrating sunset with a yoga class led by God-like people named Adonis and Electra.

Then, the class began. Electra began calling poses in Greek. It turns out that nothing in a typical Greek school curriculum prepares you for Greek translations of yoga poses. I can order coffee and donuts in Greek with the best of them. I can call taxis and find the bathroom and figure out how much a beach chair costs, all in Greek. I cannot, however, get through a yoga class. Adonis sensed the problem—more likely, he saw me flailing confusedly trying to do yoga while watching what everyone else was doing—and came to my rescue (of course he did). As Electra called the poses in Greek, he translated to English. I now seriously loved Adonis and envied Electra. This system worked out beautifully and I reveled in this Greek yoga dream I appeared to be living.

Eventually, we reached the end of class. Electra decided to lead the students through a guided relaxation, where she asked us to systematically relax one part of our bodies at a time until we were fully relaxed and could truly savor a moment of rest. She was now speaking fully in English. I guess the Greek students understood more English than I understood Greek.

Slowly, she guided us:

"Relax your toes." Pause.

"Relax your ankles."

"Relax your knees. Feel the backs of your knees settle into the mat."

"Relax your hips." Long pause.

"Relax your genitals."

Oh, boy.

I'm pretty sure I knew what she meant, but I am also 100 percent sure that was not the correct way to say what she meant in English. I think the word she was looking for was "pelvis." All I could think in that moment was, how exactly does one relax one's genitals? If I knew how to do this, I didn't think I wanted to do it in public in the middle of a beautiful yoga class in my most favorite place in the world.

And that thought struck me as the most hilarious thing I had ever thought in my entire life. So, now I had an actual problem much bigger than relaxing my genitals. I was on the verge of a complete giggle fit in a yoga class, which is definitely not appropriate. It was even less appropriate when the Olympian instructors had gone to great lengths to speak my native language to make sure I could follow their teaching.

But then I realized this was actually a lesson in the making, an opportunity to show I was a real yogi. Yoga is all about mindfulness, using your breath to get you through challenging poses and to stay as calm off the mat as you are on it. This was my moment!

I took very deep breaths. I tried desperately to listen to the non-genital words Goddess Electra was speaking. I wasn't overtly laughing, but my body was shaking with the effort to contain the giggles. I tried every yoga trick I could think of, but the giggles seemed to be winning. Desperate, I bit hard on the inside of my lip; the combination of the pain plus physically forcing my mouth shut actually worked, and the giggle crisis was successfully averted. While I don't think chomping on your lip qualifies as a yoga pose (chomp-asana?), I consider this moment to be a turning point of sorts in my yoga practice. I didn't laugh! Perhaps chomp-asana should be a new mindfulness/giggle-prevention tool.

When I returned to Santorini the following year, I discovered that Adonis and Electra had relocated their yoga studio to a bigger island. Apparently, Electra gave birth to twins in the year since I had seen them! Which may help explain why genitals were so top of mind for her after all. That and she's married to an actual Adonis.

Mitzi and the
Magic Markets

———

Kaninchen is the German word for bunny rabbit. It's also an unfortunate nickname I earned while working in a baked beans factory in central Germany. To enter the production floor, I needed to wear a one-size-fits-all white jumpsuit over my regular clothes for product safety reasons. But at 5'3" tall, the oversized jumpsuit posed a tripping hazard. It seemed totally logical to gather the extra material at the waist, inadvertently creating a poufy white bunny tail.

But perhaps I should take a step back.

Several years ago, I managed the US baked beans business for a global food manufacturer. We wanted to expand our business by bringing a breakthrough baked beans technology (yes, really) used in Europe to the US. My divorce had just been finalized, and I jumped on the opportunity to take an international assignment that no one but me and my boss needed to approve. So, that's how I ended up in a German baked beans factory dressed like a bunny. In retrospect, I think my new nickname had unanticipated advantages.

Looking ridiculous can be a great way to make friends; certainly, none of my German colleagues viewed me as corporate or intimidating. Because they wanted *Kaninchen* to enjoy her time in Germany, they brought me to the nearby town of Goslar to see the local Christmas market.

Christmas markets have been a tradition in Germany and northern Europe for hundreds of years. In the weeks of Advent, leading up to Christmas Day, city centers across Germany turn into winter wonderlands, selling local foods and handmade ornaments and providing a festive gathering place for locals and tourists as they prepare for Christmas. I was particularly intrigued by these markets because the Christmas season is my favorite time of the year, despite the cold weather. I love pretty much everything about the holidays—the music, the cookies, the decorations, the shopping, and of course, the lights. I love driving around to see Christmas trees in houses and town centers, and wreaths with lights on lampposts. My Christmas tree is so covered in lights and ornaments that you can barely see the branches. It's also been up for about five years now. It made me so sad to take it down that I just kept procrastinating. And then a few weeks went by, and then a few months . . . and now, five years. Sometimes, I'll open all my blinds and light it up in the summer just for kicks. It's probably a good thing I don't own a home or I'd end up on one of those Christmas house competition shows on HGTV, or in some sort of nasty dispute with a neighbor who actually wants to sleep at night without ten million lights shining into his window.

So, given my love of the season, I was incredibly excited to experience a literal Christmas village in Goslar. The main town square was surrounded by Tudor-style buildings, including a five-hundred-year-old hotel. Thick banners of lights crisscrossed the square, meeting at the center in an enormous circle. The square was filled with little wooden huts selling local goods—handmade Christmas ornaments and other holiday decorations. And the food! Delicious gingerbread cookies, called *lebkuchen*, sometimes covered in thin layers of chocolate. Marzipan in every shape and size you can imagine. A dense, sugar-covered pastry with candied fruit called the *Christstollen*. Bratwurst of all different sizes and origins grilling everywhere, typically on huge round grates that looked like giant wagon wheels, suspended with thick chains over fire pits. But my favorite thing was the *glühwein*—hot, mulled wine served in themed mugs that changed every year.

In a nearby square, there was even a Christmas tree forest with fifty giant, lighted Christmas trees that visitors could walk among. At one point, I sat down on a bench under one of the trees in the Christmas Forest, eating a half-meter long bratwurst—Germany's answer to foot long hot dogs—and drinking a steaming mug of *glühwein* and realized that this was the most festive I had ever felt in my entire Christmas-loving life. If it were possible to live inside the Christmas carol, "Winter Wonderland," this would be what that would feel like.

I was so delighted by my too-brief experience in Goslar that I knew I had to come back to Northern Europe to see more of these amazing holiday markets. Even though I was increasingly comfortable traveling alone and wasn't trying to coordinate with a travel partner, it still took me two years to find the time. Christmas markets are generally open only for the first few weeks of December, closing by Christmas day. I could only take off one week of work in December and, in my typical Type A fashion, I wanted to see as many markets as possible, so I needed to find a very efficient way to travel between markets. I did some research and found a one-week-long river cruise along the Danube River that seemed to solve this challenge. Stopping in six Northern European cities, travelers could hop right off the ship and into the town centers to visit all the markets! This sounded perfect, exactly what I was looking for.

In retrospect, I probably should have done some more research or paid a little more attention to the research I was doing. I was so focused on logistics that I failed to notice a few consistent themes in the advertising materials:

1. Everyone featured in the cruise materials (pictures of people enjoying time on the ship, in port, etc.) had grey hair. In fact, one picture showed a grey-haired woman sitting in the ship's library, wearing reading glasses.

2. The ship's amenities seemed rather tame. For exercise, there was a walking track. The aforementioned library and time and space to read quietly were highlighted. Entertainment included lectures, cooking demonstrations, and classical or regional music performances. I can only assume I was so relieved to not see a focus on the things I typically associate with cruises and don't like (i.e., overeating, general cheesiness), that I didn't stop to consider what demographic would most likely resonate with these types of activities.

3. Repeated focus around how passengers would be "cared for" by staff. A guide would meet you at the baggage claim when you arrived and drop you off at your gate on the return, the concierge would plan your days, guided tours were included at every port, etc.

Now, one would think that someone looking at these materials, especially someone who works in marketing for a living and is herself responsible for creating advertising materials, would draw the obvious conclusion that this trip catered to an older demographic. Somehow, this did not occur to me. Or, at least, not until I landed in Nuremberg, Germany, and headed over to the ship's meeting point near the baggage claim.

Arriving at the meeting point, I was surprised to see a large group of seemingly eager-to-help young people wearing extremely brightly colored t-shirts bearing the cruise line's logo. I was expecting to see one person with a clipboard, not an army of helpers. The Eager Army seemed equally puzzled by me, and this increased with every question I answered.

"No, I'm not traveling with anyone else." This one, I'm used to by now.

"No, I don't have any luggage to claim." Carry-on bags only for me!

"No, I don't need someone to walk me to the bath-room." Seriously?

I briefly wondered if I had entered a bizarre excessive-service-oriented parallel universe or was suffering from some sort of jetlag-induced paranoia. And then, in the distance, I spotted a caravan of very slowly moving very old people, approaching the Eager Army, whose bright shirts and bright faces stood at attention. My shipmates had begun to arrive.

I would generously say that the average age of the approaching group was about seventy-five, which was more than twice my age at the time. It took nearly an hour for the Eager Army to corral the group, making sure there were no stragglers, collect their luggage, and walk everyone to the bathroom. Finally, we meandered to the bus to take us to our ship. I was determined to be open-minded—when I get older, I don't want to be pre-judged for my age—but this group was living into every existing old-person stereotype, so staying open-minded was challenging. I tried to reassure myself with the thought that this week would be like an opportunity to spend time with my grandparents again.

That first night, we were docked in Nuremberg, so I dropped my bags in my cabin and headed right back off the ship to go to the famous Nuremberg *Christkindlmarkt*. This market was absolutely enormous. A giant fountain in the main square was surrounded by hundreds of wooden stalls selling seemingly everything. There were so many vendors that the stalls were grouped thematically—bratwurst in one section, *lebkuchen* in another, handmade ornaments somewhere else. It made navigating slightly easier. Exhausted with jetlag and overcome by excessive festive-ness, I decided to find a seat in a restaurant for dinner to try to soak in all this holiday spirit while sitting down. Almost magically, I found the most perfect tiny table for one, squeezed into a corner facing an oddly placed but giant window with an absolutely perfect view of the main square. And a perfect vantage point to watch what can best be described as a parade of aged elves playing drums. I hope it really was an old elf parade and not a *glühwein*-induced hallucination. It was an amazing start to this trip, and I was super excited for the rest of my week.

The next day, I spent more time in the Nuremberg market before we set sail for our next stop, Regensburg. That night, I decided to try dinner in the ship's restaurant, which had open seating. I sat down at an empty table and soon two couples joined me. We introduced ourselves and exchanged basic pleasantries. Not long after, the conversation went downhill.

"Today was nice, but I'm having a lot of pain in my hip after all that walking," said one of the husbands.

Uh-oh. For the record, it was not very much walking.

"What kind of hip pain?" asked the other husband. "I am a retired doctor," he explained. "Maybe I can help. Are you taking anything to help with the pain?"

What followed was a detailed, lengthy conversation about hip pain, its causes, possible implications and the wide variety of medicines and therapies capable of helping to resolve it. I sat there quietly, nodding appropriately while trying desperately to find an opening to enable a more positive—ideally, different—conversation. When I realized this would not be possible, I considered jabbing my fork in my own eye to make this conversation stop but was worried that this act might prompt a new conversation about the potential causes, implications, and medicines to help resolve a corneal abrasion. Deciding to cut my losses, I left the table as soon as politely possible and headed straight for the bar.

The next morning, the ship was sailing through the Main-Danube canal, an engineering marvel that connects the Danube and Rhine Rivers and enables river travel across Europe from the Black Sea to the North Sea. This canal contains a series of locks, which are basically water elevators that raise the water level hundreds of feet to connect the rivers. I had never sailed through a water elevator before and really wanted to see what that looked and felt like. Partly to get away from the rest of my shipmates and partly to watch the lock system in practice, I headed for the small self-service breakfast area, which had amazing floor-to-ceiling windows with 360-degree views.

Much to my relief, I was the only guest there, so I was able to eat a simple breakfast and watch the lock system close up. It was extremely cool. The locks were so narrow that I could see walls on either side of the ship. They seemed close enough to reach out a window and touch. The ship was secured inside the lock and, as water flowed in, the ship would rise. I didn't feel the lift—it was much subtler than an actual elevator—but I could see the ship's level change by watching the walls to the side move up or down. Relativity at work—of course, the ship was moving, not the walls. I'm sure my head kept swiveling back and forth as though I was watching a very slow tennis match.

At one point, mid-head-swivel, two white-haired men came into my frame of view. One was holding a camera, and they were talking very excitedly to one another.

"I can't believe you made us go to that formal breakfast. Look how amazing this is! We might have missed it!" said the shorter of the two men to the taller.

"I'm on vacation," said the taller man. "I don't want to get my own breakfast on vacation. I think that's fair. And now we can see the locks, so we both win." And then, noticing me, "Oh my goodness, honey, are we right in your way? And we're so loud. I'm so sorry! Did you have this place all to yourself?"

Not waiting for me to reply, the shorter man said, "She's *smart*! Look how amazing this is! And you need to be *served breakfast* on vacation. She has the best view in the house!"

I liked these guys immediately. After assuring them they were not blocking my view in the room of glass, we chatted for a while about locks, how none of us had ever been in a lock system before and how cool it was that we didn't feel like we were moving but could see that we were. And then, just as excitedly as they had appeared, they burst out of the room to get ready for the day's activities in the charming city of

Regensburg. I realized we hadn't even introduced ourselves with all of the lock-induced excitement.

I had an absolutely delightful day wandering the markets of Regensburg. After walking, eating, and shopping myself to a state of ecstatic exhaustion, I decided to rest with a giant mug of *glühwein*. This must happen to a lot of people because the markets come equipped with little huts where you can sit and warm up. They look just like the wooden huts where the vendors sell food and goods, but these have real fires in the middle and benches around the sides. It's brilliant. So, I sat with my back to the fire and a steaming mug of *glühwein* in my hands, watching the passers-by amidst the holiday cheer, when two familiar faces appeared.

"Hey, aren't you the girl from breakfast?" asked the taller white-haired man from breakfast. "We didn't even introduce ourselves! I'm Charles, and this is Ted. We're so curious about you! Are you by yourself? And you look younger than Ted's kids! Who are you eating dinner with on the ship?"

I introduced myself and confirmed that I was the "girl from breakfast," traveling alone, and younger than Ted's kids. I also tried to find a polite way to explain the previous night's dinner incident, but I didn't even get to the hip pain before Charles informed me that they were here to rescue me.

"We have the most fun table on the ship!" Charles assured me enthusiastically as Ted nodded in agreement. "Have dinner with us!"

How could I resist this invitation? I agreed, Charles told me where to find the fun table, and they headed out to do more exploring while I continued to drink in the holiday spirit.

Back on the ship that night, I headed to the meeting place and found Charles and Ted, as well as Stephi and Mitzi, their fun friends. A retired teacher, Stephi was in her early seventies.

Mitzi, who immediately told me she was eighty-two, was a still-practicing nurse educator. Nothing about Mitzi validated that she was eighty-two years old. She was the definition of spunky, with a vibrancy and vitality that radiated from within. She reminded me of really dry champagne—crisp, refreshing, and effervescent. I wanted to reverse adopt her. Both widowed for more than a decade, Stephi and Mitzi had been traveling together for years and had racked up a collection of adventures to share with the table. Just three nights into the trip, this foursome had already befriended all the waiters and bartenders.

As soon as we sat down, full bottles of wine appeared as well as every appetizer on the menu. "Why choose just one?" asked Charles. He somehow proactively ordered me a cheese plate that was not on the menu because, "you seem like someone who loves cheese," and a waiter actually created one and brought it to me. Charles was awesome. I was totally enamored of the whole group. Not only were they fun, as promised, but they had also lived through amazing challenges. Charles and Ted talked about what it was like to be gay in New York before you could safely be open about it. Mitzi talked about pursuing college and a career when so few women took that path. It was enlightening.

After many drinks, my tablemates started calling me Princess. I think it was because "Sara" means "Princess," but I'm honestly not entirely sure. I *am* sure that these four could drink me under the table any day. Mitzi didn't feel that "Princess" was sufficient; she thought I deserved a grander title, like Queen. Not missing a beat, Charles turned to Mitzi and said, "Honey, she can't be 'Queen.' I've been a Queen since before Princess Sara was born!" This was the first of many moments where I may have actually shot wine out of my nose from laughing. Charles was right about his fun table.

As the ship continued its journey down the Danube, I continued to spend time with my four new friends. One afternoon, the ship was sailing along the scenic Wachau Valley, Austria's famed wine region, whose shores are filled with medieval castles. Even though it was particularly cold that day, I decided to go to the rooftop deck for optimal viewing of this beautiful place. Wearing nearly everything in my suitcase and holding my scarf and hat, I ran into Mitzi on my way upstairs.

"Are you really going to sit outside while we sail?" she asked. "It's freezing!"

"It's supposed to be beautiful," I replied. "I don't want to miss it! Who knows when I'll be back?"

"You are a brave woman," Mitzi said. "I might be too old for this kind of cold."

We each continued on our way. When I got to the roof, just a few people were there because it was positively frigid. Between the cold temperature and the wind, it felt like any exposed skin was actively being exfoliated. That said, the view was breathtaking. I was sitting there for a few minutes when, much to my surprise, Mitzi appeared, also wearing what appeared to be her entire suitcase. She had decided I was right and this was too beautiful an experience to miss. Mitzi and I sat together on the roof of our ship for at least an hour, sailing along the Danube River, admiring castles and talking about life. Mitzi told me she liked me because she thought I was brave to travel alone. I thought she was brave for choosing to have a career and a husband when no one thought "having it all" was an option. She told me her secret:

"Whenever I felt uncomfortable, like people were judging me or didn't think I belonged, I would just tell myself, 'These people must not know who I am.' Because if they knew me, they would know I deserve to be here. 'They just don't know who I am.' And that would make me lift my chin a bit higher. Who are these people to judge me?"

Mitzi was truly an inspiration.

The last night of the cruise turned out to be one of the most hilariously unexpected nights of my life. After dinner, the entertainment was a Christmas carol sing-along, led by a German duo wearing lederhosen while playing, respectively, an accordion and a strange tambourine-drum on a stick. The two men weren't exactly young or fit; it looked like they had spent long lifetimes enjoying quite a lot of bratwurst, Bavarian pretzels, and beer. Fat men wearing lederhosen is kind of a spectacle in itself. To make matters worse, these guys were seriously engaged in Christmas caroling, dancing vigorously as they sang.

We drank more wine than I want to think about while singing along at the top of our lungs; it was so much fun singing with abandon with my new friends. It turns out that the singing wasn't enough to distract Charles from the duo's costumes. He wondered aloud how, with such large calves in so much motion, were these men keeping their knee socks from drooping? Mitzi turned to Charles and said, "You're worried about his *socks*? I think he's got bigger problems. I bet his dumplings are drooping, too!"

I completely lost it. I am pretty sure that this was the hardest I had laughed all year, possibly for many years. It was that kind of laugh where you can't breathe or make any sound except for the occasional high-pitched squeal when you do successfully manage to inhale. I am absolutely certain that when I booked my trip to see the Christmas markets, I had no idea I'd find myself singing Christmas carols with senior citizens while my octogenarian hero made lewd jokes about dumplings.

My Christmas market river cruise was definitely memorable, if unexpected. In addition to eating my way through the most festive places on earth at my favorite time of year, I learned a lot about how I want to age—joyfully and with purpose, like Mitzi. From the initial trepidation at the baggage claim and the disastrous hip-pain-themed dinner to that final night, laughing with my new "senior" friends, I gained an entirely new perspective. Certainly, my new friends had experienced difficulties and challenges in their lives, and were experiencing them now, but they chose not to let those challenges weigh them down and to instead see every day as an opportunity for joy. It was inspiring and created a whole new model for me about what aging means. If I lose my confidence along the journey, I'll think of Mitzi, lift my chin up and say to myself, "They just don't know who I am." And I'll picture that vibrant eighty-two-year-old with her arms akimbo and a sparkle in her eye, and I'll smile.

Two and a Half Years Later

Waiting on a street corner in Santorini for my adopted Greek "parents" to pick me up for dinner, a German couple I'd never met joined me. Bi-annual Santorini visitors for the past twenty years, they had also become friends of my adopted family. It was the last day of their visit to Santorini and the first day of mine that year, so our Greek family thought it would be nice to celebrate our favorite island together.

During a lovely dinner overlooking Vlychada, a casual and not-touristy port on the southern tip of the island, I asked Frieda where she was from in Germany.

"I grew up in a small town in central Germany; you would never hear about it in the States," she said.

"I used to travel to central Germany for work a few years ago," I told her, thinking it best to avoid all mention of baked beans or my German nickname. "There was a beautiful Christmas market in a town called Goslar that I loved."

"Goslar?" she exclaimed. "You've been to Goslar?" She looked stunned.

"Yes, it was beautiful! I have a themed *glühwein* mug with the Christmas Forest on it!"

"Goslar is my hometown! I can't believe you've been there."

I mean really, what are the odds that an American woman and a German couple would find themselves at dinner on a Greek island with shared friends in the first place? That one summer, our visits overlapped by one day, and on that one day, we met and discovered our shared love of their beautiful hometown at Christmas. Statistically highly improbable? Yes. Delightful? Also, yes. Moments like these make me feel like my choices are validated and that I am exactly where I'm supposed to be—reminding me how small the world really is.

Studies Show, I'm
an Asshole

———

"Can you believe that asshole? He just cut me off! Oh, of course he did. He's driving a BMW!"

Growing up, my mother always told me that BMW drivers were assholes. Whenever a BMW driver cut her off on the highway or otherwise misbehaved on the road, confirming these low expectations, she would aggressively voice her disgust. Many cars that were not actually BMWs became BMWs in the eyes of my mother when their drivers behaved badly on the road. Not surprisingly, no one in my family owned a BMW, or even considered buying one. Also not surprisingly, I married a man with a similar viewpoint. Although, in retrospect, I think his concerns were more financial than philosophical. While he was consistently opposed to spending too much money on anything, he was arguably more comfortable with assholes than my mother, given, for example, his perspective on fidelity.

When I bought my first car, BMWs weren't even remotely in my consideration set. First, I think my husband would have had a convulsive fit if I seriously suggested we spend unnecessary money on a luxury car. Second, it never occurred to me that I deserved really nice things like fancy cars. Taking care of myself had always been a very pragmatic thing—having clothes to wear and food to eat and some room in my budget to entertain myself—a belief my husband reinforced. The idea of treating myself, or buying myself nice things for the pure joy of experiencing those nice things, was entirely foreign to me and effective sacrilege to my husband. From his perspective, we already had a "primary" car—his solid, respectable sedan. He perceived my car as a backup to his, for my shorter commute. Given this, my criteria at the time for a car were very clear:

1. Functional

2. Cheap

3. Cute as possible while still meeting criteria (1) and (2)

Armed with these priorities, I made a very pragmatic purchase: a subcompact hatchback that was insanely fuel efficient. And when I say, "I," I really mean my husband. I stood by silently while he spoke with the car salesman about what I was looking for in a car, and then I signed the paperwork when it came time to actually pay. Anyway, she (I think of cars as female) was purple, so I named her Violet.

For the record, I'm not crazy for naming my car. Nicholas Epley, a University of Chicago professor, says that naming your car is an example of anthropomorphism, the act of giving human attributes to non-human objects. Apparently, anthropomorphism is a "byproduct of possessing an intelligent social awareness" and is "a reflection of our brain's greatest ability rather than a sign of our stupidity" (Elsom, 2017). Anthropomorphism was also a very cool word to bandy about when anyone mocked me about Violet's name.

In many ways, my relationship with Violet mimicked my marriage. Initially, I adored her. She was cute and fun and easy. Eventually, I came to realize that she was actually quite flawed. It turns out that fuel-efficient subcompact hatchbacks are awesome for short-distance driving in perfect weather but are downright dangerous otherwise. The car was basically a glorified go-kart that weighed about ten pounds. High winds would blow me across the road, and please, don't even get me started about driving in snow; let's just say I saw my life flash before my eyes multiple times. Also, Violet had almost zero horsepower, and correspondingly, absolutely no ability to accelerate quickly, making merging onto highways a white-knuckled experience every time. I spent so much time praying for my life and the lives of other motorists around me while driving that I am pretty sure I could have had Violet consecrated as an official house of worship. After my husband and our reliable sedan left, I tried to make my relationship with Violet last as long as I could, but after a few years, I was ready to make a change and stop risking my life on a daily basis. Plus, things were going well in my career, so it felt like a good time to make a big purchase.

This time, I had a long list of car criteria. Small, but not too small. Not a sedan—I just don't like them. Not a truck—they're too big and too tall, and I don't want to flash people getting in or out of my car when I wear dresses. What I really wanted was a slightly larger, much heavier, and more comfortable version of Violet. Which, it seemed, did not exist. Until I saw a TV commercial introducing the new to the US market BMW X1, the most perfect car for me. I stopped in my tracks when I saw this commercial; I stood up and stared at the TV and immediately googled this car. It's not that the commercial was so great (sorry, BMW marketers), but it was advertising exactly the specific thing I wanted but was convinced did not exist. I was thrilled! The X1 was a small, all-wheel-drive hatchback. Google quickly confirmed that it weighed almost twice as much as Violet. It was perfect!

But I had one tiny problem: The BMW X1 is a BMW. BMW drivers are assholes, right? BMWs are expensive luxury cars; did I really need to spend so much money to buy a luxury car and, potentially, become an asshole? It all felt too indulgent, so I decided to do some research.

I polled my friends at work and realized that several of them owned BMWs and were not assholes. Also, they really liked their cars and did not fear for their lives while driving. Armed with these insights, I decided to test drive the X1. Doing so was a revelation. When I drove this car, I was in absolute love. Not only did it meet all my criteria, but also it was *fast*. And I could actually accelerate to safely merge onto a highway without fearing for my life. I could even drive up hilly roads without the car whining and hiccupping in protest. This was beyond exciting. I read about every bell and whistle and picked out the exact configuration of car that I wanted. And then I broke the news to my parents.

"So, I finally decided I'm going to buy a new car!"

"It's about time! Violet is not safe! I still can't believe your stupid ex-husband stranded you in Pittsburgh, with that big house and no family and a dangerous car. . ."

I clearly needed to cut my mom off before this turned into an ex-husband bashing. Also, I anticipated that the news of my impending asshole status might be almost as emotionally problematic.

"Yes, yes, exactly! So, I am getting a different car, a much heavier one!"

"Heavier?" my dad piped in. He was apparently listening on speaker. "Are you buying a pickup truck?"

"What? Of course not. How would I get in a pickup truck while wearing dresses without flashing people?"

Laughing, he asked, "How do you know how much the car weighs?" Apparently, most people don't care that much about the weight of the car they are about to purchase. But seriously, if you had nearly been blown off the George Washington Bridge trying to drive into New York City during a storm, you'd care about how much your new car weighed, too.

"I googled it!" I was triumphant. "This car weighs almost twice as much as Violet!"

Still laughing, now harder, "Well, you've done your research! What car is this that meets your weight requirements?"

"Well, it's a small, all-wheel drive hatchback. It's new on the US market!" I was stalling. How do you tell your parents that you are a prospective asshole?

"Which one?"

"Well, it's a BMW. The X1. It's a small hatchback!"

There was an awkward pause. Mom jumped in first.

"You know BMW drivers are assholes, right? Do you really want to be an asshole?"

"At least they're safe assholes," Dad offered. "Maybe because their cars are so heavy?"

I managed to reassure my parents that I would be both safer and not an asshole in my new BMW.

Now I just had to figure out how to get my new car. I decided I wanted to buy, not lease. Then I did extensive online research to figure out what I should actually pay for this car and built a massive spreadsheet to lay out my options. What can I say? I'm an ex-banker math geek. This is how I roll.

Despite my extensive preparation, it still took me three tries to buy my car. The first salesman just flat-out refused to negotiate with me. He kept calling me "sweetie" and telling me how pretty the car would look with me driving it. I wish I were kidding. Furious, I tried a second dealership. That one was a marginally better experience. The salesman there wasn't totally patronizing; he was just dishonest. Claimed he would "make me a deal" on a higher-end option than I wanted and wasted an entire afternoon of my life that I'll never get back not doing so. I would like to think these experiences were not a function of me being a single woman negotiating on her own, but I guess I'll never really know.

For obvious reasons, I was slightly enraged by the time I got to the third dealership. But this time, I had an extra piece of information that I was sure would help my negotiations. This third dealer had a database online where I could research available inventory. I wanted a very specific version of the X1, in a very specific funky blue color. As luck would have it, this third dealership had exactly one of exactly the car in exactly the color that I wanted. And I was determined to get it.

I went in with guns (spreadsheets?) blazing, which it turned out was pretty unnecessary. The salesman seemed pretty happy to get rid of the one funky blue X1 on his lot and, after a half-hearted attempt to make me pay a stupid price, came back with a number lower than the lowest number on my spreadsheet. I was delighted and agreed happily, instantly returning to my normal, bubbly self. The salesman was extremely confused. He later told me that I "freaked him out" when I "went bipolar" and transformed from raging to smiling right before his eyes. But he was happy to make the sale and, a few days later, I picked up my new funky blue BMW X1.

The second I sat in my new car, I was in whatever is the opposite of buyer's remorse. I *loved* this car. I named her Bluebell. Driving Bluebell was pure joy, and every time I looked at her, I felt proud. It was kind of strange to feel such delight about buying what was really just an entry-level luxury car, so I spent some time reflecting and came up with the following reasons why buying Bluebell was so pivotal for me:

1. Being able to buy this car suggested some measure of hard-fought success.

2. The car was a symbol that I was worthy of having nice things and taking kind care of myself. She wasn't just any car to get me from point A to point B but something more special, which wasn't a necessity, but made driving a pleasure.

3. I did it all myself—from that first moment of seeing the TV ad (TV ads still work!) and figuring out what specifically I wanted and how much I was willing to pay for it to negotiating and actually paying for it.

So, to me, Bluebell represented a tangible symbol of my accomplishment, value, and independence—something I earned through years of hard work and perseverance. It didn't matter that other people had "better," fancier cars. I earned this one and she was exactly what I wanted. And that's what I continue to see every time I look at her.

And then one night I was scrolling through my Facebook feed and came across a link to this *Wall Street Journal*

MarketWatch video: "BMW Drivers Really Are Jerks, Studies Find."

Uh-oh.

According to this video, several studies in both the US and the UK confirm that BMW drivers are jerks. In the US, one study tested how drivers behaved when a pedestrian crossed the street in a crosswalk. While drivers are supposed to stop for pedestrians, and most did, BMW drivers were the least likely to stop. Another US study assessed driver behavior at four-way intersections. Again, BMW drivers were the most likely to drive through these intersections out of turn. And in the UK, study participants were asked to note the drivers and cars that they most associated with aggressive driving and/or road rage. The study found that "men between the ages of thirty-five and fifty driving a blue BMW were most likely to engage in road-rage behaviors such as aggressive driving and swearing."

In summary, BMW drivers are jerks, and drivers of blue BMWs are the jerkiest of all. Given that my Bluebell is, rather obviously, *blue*, this study finding is quite unfortunate for me. As Tom Bemis concludes in the video, "BMW touts its cars as 'the ultimate driving machines.' Perhaps they should add, 'for the ultimate jerks.'"

So, it turns out that Mom was right all along. As for me, although I am statistically an "ultimate jerk," I am doing my best to not be an asshole. In fact, I actively overcompensate for my blue BMW by being an especially nice driver. I always stop for pedestrians in crosswalks, wait my turn at four-way intersections, and avoid road-rage behaviors. I'm hoping for a different outcome the next time they do a study.

Through the Water Glass

I think there are some things in life we are just not meant to understand. The older I get, the more convinced I am of this, and the more amazed I am by the seemingly impossible coincidences and bizarre connections between disparate events that I experience. Strangely, cats seem to be a mechanism the Universe uses to enlighten me.

I recently adopted a black and white tuxedo cat and named him Loukoumaki, a Greek term of endearment that loosely translates into "little sweetie." This is most definitely not a typical name for an American cat and seems to be entirely unpronounceable by the veterinary community. The story of how Loukoumaki got his name proves that T.S. Eliot was onto something when he wrote that "the naming of cats is a difficult matter."

One summer, I was vacationing in Greece and started thinking that my next cat needed a Greek name. Given that I love Greece and have no children to name, it seemed perfectly appropriate to have a Greek-named cat. I thought about some of my favorite Greek words, but nothing felt right to me.

And then, while in a taxi on the way to my favorite winery on the island, it occurred to me: *loukoumades. Loukoumades* are these amazing fried donut balls, typically smothered in honey and cinnamon, that were sent down from Heaven (Olympus?) to delight Greeks everywhere. Seriously, they are amazing. I consider *loukoumades* to be on par with democracy and architectural marvels like the Parthenon in terms of amazing things for which the world should thank the Greeks. However, "*Loukoumades*" didn't seem like a good cat name. For starters, it's plural. It seemed weird to name a cat "Donuts" as opposed to "Donut." The singular form, *loukoumas*, sounds plural to an American even though it isn't, so that didn't work either. But I figured there must be some derivative of "*loukoumades*" that could work as a name. As I arrived at the winery, I made a mental note to ask my Greek friends about this.

Settled into the tasting room, with samples of twelve wines to taste, I reveled in my amazing surroundings. The tasting room was really more like a giant pergola than an actual room. On the flat side of Santorini, the back side opposite the famed dramatic cliffs, it was surrounded by vineyards with a perfect view of the Aegean Sea and several islands in the distance. Alongside a sleek indoor wine shop, the outdoor patio was complete with fig trees and vibrant bougainvillea. As I tasted the wines, I could feel the soft sea breezes.

Sitting beneath the fig trees, eating local delicacies like white eggplant and fava while drinking, in my opinion, the best wines from the island was a truly magical way to spend an afternoon. Maximizing my delight, several cats lived on the winery grounds. I was particularly charmed by a darling black and white kitten who was trying to make friends with all of my fellow wine-tasters. She eventually worked her way over to me and head-butted my leg, the universal sign of kitty affection. Of course, I had to pet her. The amused waitress stopped by my table, laughing.

"That cat is making friends with everyone!" she exclaimed.

"I love her! She's so sweet!" I said.

"We think so, too! That's why we named her Loukoumaki!"

I mean, seriously, what are the odds of this?

"Loukoumaki?" I asked incredulously.

"Yes, Loukoumaki! When you add 'aki' to the end of a Greek word, it means it's small. So, we are saying that she is little and sweet!"

So that was how the Universe informed me of the name for my next cat, in the most bizarre way possible.

My American Loukoumaki cat makes up in sweetness what he lacks in littleness. He's pretty big for a cat, which is largely my fault. Turns out both Greeks and Italians are good at fattening up the ones they love. Most interestingly, Lou—as I call him for short, and to make my vet feel more comfortable—doesn't seem to realize he's a cat. He greets me excitedly at the door when I come home. He chases his own tail. He fetches. He is also really laid-back and eager to please. He scratches what he is supposed to scratch, occasionally responds to his name, and almost never causes any mischief. Honestly, it wouldn't surprise me too much if he started barking someday.

As such, Lou is remarkably different from my previous black and white cat, Chapstick—so named because she reminded me of a ChapStick tube when she stood up on her back legs. Chapstick was tiny, barely eight pounds, with a personality inversely proportionate to her size. The only vet Chapstick ever liked described her personality as "spicy," and she was being nice. Chapstick adored me but was otherwise hell-bent on destruction and causing mischief at every turn. In particular, she was on a mission to eviscerate any loaf of bread that entered my home, knock over all vases filled with flowers and water (empty vases were never bothered), and to drink exclusively from my water glass even though she always had a full bowl of her own, much to my dismay. I love cats but not sharing beverages with them.

I never understood the bread thing. She once dragged a whole loaf of bread all the way across the apartment to her litter box, where she ripped the whole thing, loaf of bread and bag, to complete shreds. Not even a month before she passed away at fifteen years old, she managed to jump on the kitchen counter despite her arthritis and triumphantly destroy a slice of bread I was planning to toast. To this day, I automatically rush to put away the bread as soon as I get home from the grocery store, think twice before buying flowers, and guard my water glass from kitty thievery, and it always makes me a little sad and nostalgic when I remember that bread, flowers, and water actually have nothing to fear these days in my home.

On the day that would have been Chapstick's sixteenth birthday, I thought it would be a nice tribute to take a look through a photo album of my favorite pictures of her. I grabbed the album and a glass of water and settled in on the sofa to reflect on fifteen years with my amazing cat. It was incredible to look back on those years; so much had changed in my life, but Chapstick was such a constant force. I could still feel her energy and personality radiating from the photos. Single me, married me, divorced me. Pudgy me, fat me, thin me—but my Chapstick was the same, full of life and mischief, making me happy on my worst days. Feeling really grateful for our time together, I smiled and looked up from the photo album.

At that exact moment, Lou unexpectedly jumped up on the coffee table, walked purposefully across it, made clear eye contact with me, and started *drinking from my water glass*, something he had never done before and has never done since. I stared at him in shock. Somehow it seemed to me that Lou looked equally surprised to find himself drinking my water. I will never understand how it's possible, but I like to think Chapstick made him do it. She always knew the best way to get my attention. I think I will leave a loaf of bread out for her seventeenth birthday, just to see what happens.

Dead Sea Diving

U n-becoming a Wall Street banker in favor of the greener pastures of brand management has turned out to be the most significant career decision of my life so far. One of the perks of working in brand is the travel, which typically offsets the infrequent pangs of regret that surface when my still-banker friends buy multimillion-dollar homes in beautiful Connecticut towns. Some of the business reasons for this travel are dubious at best. I've been sent to Germany to explore baked beans manufacturing technology, London and New Zealand to shoot TV commercials, Barcelona to attend a global meeting, and Montreal to more deeply understand a competitive brand.

And this is in addition to frequent domestic travel to supervise brand mentions on talk shows, help salespeople sell products, and watch consumers from behind two-way mirrors. I'm actually starting to wonder if travel is part of my compensation. Sure, I don't make as much money as I would if I were still a banker, but I have so many frequent flyer miles that Delta staff actually greet me by name on flights to ask for my feedback.

One of my most surprising business trips was an all-expenses-paid culinary immersion and tour through Israel.

A business reason was actually offered for this seemingly extravagant trip. I worked for a company that makes and sells hummus in the US. Most Americans didn't grow up eating hummus and a surprisingly large percentage of the population (almost 70 percent of households) doesn't buy it. In Israel, hummus is a staple and is eaten for all meals in a variety of ways that would be quite unusual to the average American. The idea was to send a bunch of Americans who sell hummus to the place that sells the most hummus per capita so they could understand more about how to sell more hummus at home. Plausible? I guess so. An extremely cool job perk for sure.

I approached this trip with a blend of excitement and trepidation. On the excitement side, I had always wanted to see Jerusalem and the Dead Sea, which we would visit on the trip, and I was interested in better understanding the origins of hummus. I also love food, and discovering new (to me) foods and experiencing culture through food are two of my favorite things about travel. On the other hand, I do watch the news. It was hard not to be aware of the tensions in Israel, and in Jerusalem in particular. I kept reminding myself of the reasons to be excited and reassuring myself with the idea that surely my company wouldn't put me and nine colleagues in harm's way. Plus, I wasn't sure I would have ventured to Israel on a solo trip, so this was an opportunity to see a place I might not have otherwise seen.

Upon arriving in Tel Aviv, my colleagues and I were immediately whisked off to a kickoff dinner with our CEO. In general, I wouldn't recommend engaging in conversations with the CEO of one's company while extremely jet-lagged, but at least my colleagues and I were all in the same largely incoherent boat. It's also not optimal to meet your group's two armed bodyguards while jet-lagged; my foggy brain noodled for hours about whether to be grateful they were there and armed or alarmed that they were needed in the first place. Also concerning was that only one of the bodyguards was introduced as such; he was obviously armed and carrying a mysterious backpack. The other one was technically introduced as our group's photographer (um, why did we need a photographer?), but he was carrying a gun in his back pocket. I read between the lines and concluded that he was bodyguard number two. Really, none of this should be sorted out while jet-lagged in a foreign country and attempting to say smart business things to one's colleagues. It seemed like a great time to drink some wine and eat some real hummus to distract myself.

The next few days that followed were an intense whirlwind of hummus-eating, factory-touring, and market-visiting. I ate more pita bread than I would have thought possible. Pita bread in Israel is a revelation—none of that thin, dry stuff they sell in most grocery stores in the US. In Israel, pita bread is thick and warm and fluffy, like a cross between a flattened dinner roll and a savory pancake that you can hold in your hand. Heavenly. I also discovered a deep and abiding love of tahini, which may be the most perfect dipping sauce and condiment on earth.

Wandering through Tel Aviv's food and spice markets, I tried amazing foods that I had never heard of before but am now determined to find again. Some of my favorites included *shakshuka*, a simple hot dish of eggs poached in a sauce made with tomatoes, peppers, and onions that is eaten with fresh farm-style bread, and *burekas*, various combinations of potatoes, meats and eggs deep fried in phyllo and stuffed in a warm pita with tahini. It was kind of like a Middle Eastern turducken. The food was absolutely amazing and diverse and astonishingly fresh.

My biggest problem was the coffee. I was super excited to see what looked like Greek coffee on menus everywhere. It was called Turkish coffee, but it looked Greek to me. Except that, in most parts of Israel, Turkish coffee was Greek coffee polluted with cardamom, my least favorite spice on earth. I absolutely hate cardamom. I think it tastes like lotion. I'll never forget the time I bought what looked like an enormous cinnamon roll in a coffee shop in Stockholm, only to take a huge bite and discover it was filled with cardamom. Yuck. The most disgusting bite I've ever taken, made even worse by the fact that my brain was expecting cinnamon (my favorite spice). Every time delicious Greek coffee was ruined with cardamom, I cried a little inside. From a dietary perspective, I was overfed and undercaffeinated.

Aside from the food, everything in Israel was extreme; I could feel the intensity everywhere. Israelis get very close to each other when they talk, and they talk with passion, even if it's just about hummus. I have a big Italian family and I spend a lot of time in Italy and Greece, so I am used to passionate people, but this was a different, more aggressive type of passionate. Everyone is family and everyone looks out for each other, which is really quite lovely, but there's an almost military aspect to this intense caring. You can feel the pain of the past in the air but also the determination to move forward while never forgetting. It's a real blend of cultures—Russian, Polish, German, Austrian, Middle Eastern, Tunisian—showing itself in fascinating food and art and architecture.

As amazing as it all was, I kind of felt like I was in the center of a tornado the whole time—so much coming at me so fast that I had no real way to process anything separately.

It was everything all at once in a giant blur. I learned a ton and had lots of great ideas to take back to work when I got home. I also drank way too much wine with my colleagues and learned the hard way that being hungover on a factory floor with rotating conveyor belts is an extremely bad idea. One interesting thing I realized was that I was the only single person on this trip. In business settings, I often find that most of my colleagues are partnered, but in this situation, removed from our normal lives, my single status felt highlighted in mostly good ways. I personally witnessed the complexities that my partnered colleagues dealt with—frequent calls home, the guilt they described feeling for having an adventure while their partners handled home life alone. A few went so far as to bring their spouses on the trip with us, which created its own set of challenges for them. This was, after all, a work trip. Partners who joined had to either join us on work-related activities like factory tours or make their own plans. I felt grateful not to have to worry about any of this and just be free to have this once-in-a-lifetime experience.

Finally, the day arrived for our visit to Jerusalem and the Dead Sea. As we approached Jerusalem in our shuttle bus, I was surprised to see giant billboards advertising a big shopping mall and then, the shopping mall itself. In my mind, I think I expected the entire journey to look like a scene straight out of the Bible, so the contrast of modern life outside the Old City walls was a bit jarring. We were dropped off at the Jaffa Gate and headed straight to the Church of the Holy Sepulchre. I still get the chills thinking about that experience. I believe religion is personal and everyone has a right to their beliefs, and I wasn't sure what, if anything I would feel in this sacred place. Even though I grew up Catholic, I also didn't really understand what I was about to see.

The Church of the Holy Sepulchre was built over two sacred places in the Christian faith—Golgotha, where Jesus was crucified, and the tomb where He was buried after the Crucifixion. I knew what these two places were but didn't understand that they were *inside* this enormous Church itself.

We visited three weeks before Easter and were surrounded by thousands of pilgrims of all faiths as we entered. Between its enormous size and blend of architectural styles after centuries of renovation and reconstruction, the Church was wildly disorienting. Our tour guide was attempting to keep us together and on schedule, so she whisked us past the crowds at the entrance and directed us to climb a steep metal staircase. I was the first in our group to walk up the stairs and was trying to move quickly to keep the tour guide's pace.

As I approached the top of the stairs, I felt a crushing weight on my shoulders, as if two invisible hands were pushing me. I couldn't catch my breath or coordinate my legs to move. I remember feeling baffled; no way was I hungover, and I had no idea what was happening to me. I focused on willing my limbs to carry me the rest of the way up the stairs and not blocking the path for the rest of the group. When I arrived at the top of the staircase, I stumbled out of the way and attempted to recover. With my hands on my thighs, bent slightly at the waist, taking slow deep breaths, I realized I was crying. In front of me was a golden altar with iconic images of the Crucifixion, above a glass-encased stone. One of my colleagues, Mary, grabbed my arm. She looked just as bad as I felt.

Our tour guide clapped her hands to get the group's attention. She was now standing in front of the golden altar. Mary still had a tight grip on my arm.

Gesturing to the altar, our tour guide said, "This is the area believed to be Golgotha. It is believed that Jesus was crucified here."

Mary gasped, and we exchanged meaningful glances. I never discuss religion at work, but here I was, having a literal religious experience with my colleague.

"Are you okay?" I asked her, feeling seriously unsteady on my feet and shocked by the enormity of this experience.

"I'm not sure," she said haltingly. "Are you?"

"I'm Catholic," I responded, as if that made sense.

"Me, too," she said and hugged me.

This might go down as the most intense experience and conversation I will ever have with a colleague. We really bonded that morning, which turned out to be good prep for our visit to the Dead Sea that afternoon.

We spent a few more hours in Jerusalem, exploring more of the city's religiously charged sites, eating more hummus, and trying to find coffee free of cardamom. We walked along the Via Dolorosa, the path Jesus walked to the Crucifixion, in reverse order, from the Church of the Holy Sepulchre to the Muslim Quarter. We visited the Western Wall and paid our respects there. As we walked, we stopped to visit local shops and food stalls.

If I thought Tel Aviv was intense, Jerusalem was a whole new frightening level of intense. It was emotionally exhausting, as religious experiences met culture clashes on every corner. I had never been anywhere like this before, where I was simultaneously so curious to stay and see more but incredibly anxious to leave.

After what felt like an eternity, it was time to go to the Dead Sea for some swimming and relaxing. The Dead Sea is the lowest place on earth—its surface and shores are well over one thousand feet below sea level. The water is so salty that animals and plants can't live in it (hence the name) and everything floats, including people like me who can't swim. I was really looking forward to seeing yet another place I had read about all of my life, especially one so unusual. Also, I wanted to experience floating on water without any flotation devices.

On the drive from Jerusalem to the Dead Sea, we were given the following instructions for swimming:

- Always wear your water shoes

- Face away from the water, toward the shore

- Walk slowly, backward, into the water

- Once the water reaches the backs of your thighs, sit down into the water as if it were a chair

- Do not flip over or get water in your eyes

The only part of this that made any sense to me was the part about not getting salty water in my eyes. I am certain I have been told hundreds of times that it's a bad idea to face away from a body of water in case a wave comes up behind you and knocks you down. I had a tour guide in Hawaii who would yell at anyone who looked away from the water for even a second and tell us that Pele, the Hawaiian Goddess of Fire, would get us if we weren't paying attention. Clearly, he made an impression. Although I am not actually sure if there are waves in the Dead Sea. And how do you sit in water like it's a chair? That said, it didn't seem like the right time to suddenly turn into a rule breaker.

Arriving at the Dead Sea, we walked past a bar bearing the sign "The Lowest Bar in the World" and headed to the changing rooms. On the plus side, men and women had separate changing facilities. That is unfortunately where the plus side ended. I was really happy I was wearing my bathing suit under my clothes because the women's changing room felt like one you might see in a high school gym. It looked like renovations were in progress, but the facilities at that time included a shared room with lockers along the outside wall for your clothes and other belongings, next to a shared shower room with loosely divided shower stalls and no clear area to put the clothes you wanted to change into where they would stay dry. I think all of this would have been fine if I was on a trip with family or friends, or even by myself, but this was a business trip. I generally think it's best not to shower with and change in front of one's colleagues (call me crazy). I decided to stay focused on swimming and deal with the shower situation later.

I headed for the sea, water shoes on my feet and instructions on my mind. I turned to face the shore and began slowly walking backward. As I got closer to the water, the sand below me started to feel like glue; my feet felt like they were getting stuck in mud as I tried to move. Eventually, I reached a point where I could feel the water on my ankles, then the backs of my knees, then the backs of my thighs. I took a deep breath, sat down, and experienced complete cognitive dissonance.

It looked like water, but it felt like some sort of strange, spring-like plasma was forcefully pushing me upward. It was like doing yoga on my back with a slightly possessed magic carpet water mat with a mind of its own. The magic carpet water mat tried to flip me over, and just like in yoga, I focused on my core to stabilize myself. Eventually, I managed some sort of bizarre floating boat pose on my butt in the water, with my hands, feet and, luckily, my face, all up in the air. For about twenty minutes, I was extremely excited to be both afloat and without water in my eyes, until I realized that nearly every part of my body in the water felt like it was on fire from all the salt. I had had enough, and it was time to get out! Except, how exactly was I supposed to do that? I couldn't force my feet down into the ground without flipping over. So, I got creative. I used my hands as rudders to turn myself around so my head was facing the shore and basically flapped my way backward like a clumsy seal until my butt hit the beach and I could count gravity as a friend once more. And then I made a dash for the locker room to shower off.

But now I could no longer ignore the shared shower problem. I obviously needed to shower since my skin was muddy and also felt like I had bathed in hydrochloric acid. I also wanted to avoid being naked with my colleagues. Unfortunately, I couldn't think of a solution that would achieve both objectives. And that is how I ended up naked with my female colleagues in a shared shower by the Dead Sea on a business trip. You know, just a typical day at the office. Clearly, I needed a drink at "The Lowest Bar in the World" to top off this experience.

Taking a seat at the bar, I asked what was on tap. The bartender told me the options: Heineken and a beer with a Hebrew name I had never heard of before and could not pronounce. Embracing the authenticity of the moment, I asked for a "not-Heineken," which the bartender thought was hilarious. Mary joined me, and we toasted our emotional day with a pair of not-Heinekens.

So much of what makes travel rewarding is the opportunity to step outside of yourself, outside of your comfort zone, and experience the world in a new way. I was pretty much out of my comfort zone on every step of this trip—traveling with armed bodyguards, having physically moving religious experiences, discovering the joy of culture through unexpected foods, and feeling the pain of deep-rooted cultural tensions, practicing floating yoga, and even engaging in semipublic nudity. This was definitely a lesson in openness and taking risks.

While it's debatable how much my ability to market hummus improved, I now have a much broader perspective on what it really means to bond with your colleagues. I just hope to avoid showering with them in the future.

Kept Women in Umbria

Dashing into yoga class after a frustrating day in the office, I noticed a poster on the door advertising a yoga retreat at a rustic farming community in the central Italian countryside. Immediately, I decided this sign was a *sign* and that I would go on this retreat. I love yoga. I love Italy. What could possibly go wrong?

My yoga studio has several locations in three extremely wealthy towns in southern Connecticut. Since I work during the day, I usually go to early morning, evening, or weekend classes. The people I know from my classes are like me—working women and men, some with families, some not. On the few occasions I attended weekday classes (e.g., vacation days or work holidays), I noticed, but hadn't really internalized, that the other class attendees were quite different. These classes had pretty much no men—just perfectly maintained women with perfect designer yoga gear, perfect hair, and perfect makeup. It was especially amazing because I practice hot yoga and have no idea how to keep makeup on my face during a high-energy class in a room heated to one hundred degrees, but these women somehow did.

Pre- and post-class, all conversation seemed to focus on their children and the nannies caring for them while they practiced yoga, as well as the many trials and tribulations of managing nannies. Apparently, "nanny poaching"—the act of trying to steal someone else's nanny—is a serious concern around here. I recall some passing thoughts about how incredibly different these women's lives were from mine. I don't have a husband or kids or a nanny (obviously), and I have no desire to figure out how to apply makeup in a way that can survive hot yoga. Beyond that, I never really gave much thought to them at all until I found myself in rural Italy surrounded by ten of them.

Arriving at Rome's Fiumicino Airport, I waited at the meeting point for the rest of the group. From there, a shuttle bus would take us on the three-hour drive north to the town of Umbertide in the Umbria region, just outside of Tuscany. Slowly, the rest of the group arrived—along with more luggage than I had ever seen in my entire life. One woman had actually brought three enormous checked bags, plus a carry-on suitcase and a purse. When I say "enormous," I mean that each of these checked bags was so large that an adult human could easily fit inside without leveraging any yoga-derived flexibility. I am not sure I even own enough household items to fill this many huge suitcases, yet this was what one fellow retreater had brought to sustain herself *on retreat* for *one week*. I later learned that one of these bags contained a complete bedding set, including a down comforter, because who doesn't travel with her down comforter on an international trip to Italy in the fall? I mean, seriously.

While not quite as ludicrous, the rest of the women also had not packed lightly. I am a bit militant about packing lightly, so it's not really a fair comparison, but I had brought one carry-on suitcase and a small shoulder bag. And I was staying in Italy for an extra week after the retreat ended to explore Naples, where my family is from. I tried to keep an open mind and not be judgmental about other people's travel styles.

My intention not to judge was quickly tested. Not surprisingly, the women couldn't manage their vast quantities of luggage. Surprisingly, they seemed puzzled that no one was there to handle it for them. With ridiculous team effort, we rounded up enough carts to help us push this absurd quantity of luggage the short distance to the shuttle bus. Imagine a caravan of loud American women pushing twelve overloaded luggage carts along the causeway outside the airport; we were drawing bad attention, which I hate to do when I travel abroad.

The bus driver looked absolutely astounded as we rolled up to the bus. He was clearly playing a worrying game of mental Tetris, trying to figure out how to fit all this luggage into the back of a relatively small bus while the ladies chattered away, oblivious to the challenge they had created. As he loaded all of the bags into the bus, grunting with the effort, the bus driver gave us that look—the look Europeans give awful American tourists—and I was mortified. I pride myself in blending in when I travel and consider myself an ambassador for "good" American tourists everywhere. Creating a giant spectacle in a European airport seemed like an inauspicious beginning for this part of my Italian adventure.

Once seated on the bus, I tried to get to know the rest of the group, which was not so easy. It turned out that most of the other women knew each other; their kids went to the same private school in Greenwich. I'm a pretty decent conversationalist, and most people would say I'm very friendly, so I'm generally good at small talk and meeting new people. I can usually find common interests and mutually agreeable topics of conversation, but my efforts here fell flat. Of course, conversation requires both parties to be willing to converse and find commonalities. These ladies did not want to converse with me; that much became clear. Especially because one topic of conversation that I have not yet mastered is your children that I have never met. And that happened to be the only topic these women were willing to talk about. This was how a typical conversation went:

"Hi! I'm Sara. It's so nice to meet you! How are you doing?"

"I'm so tired after traveling and I can't believe we had to bring our luggage to the bus. They should have had someone to help us. I need to text my nanny to see how my kids are doing without me. How are your kids?"

"I don't have any kids."

"You don't? What does your husband have to say about that?"

Confused and slightly appalled, I said, "Husband? I don't have one of those, either."

"I don't know many single women in Greenwich."

Now, I was completely confused. "I don't live in Greenwich."

Making a slightly disgusted facial expression, similar to the one my cat makes when I try a new perfume, like she was worried that "inappropriate" poor people may be on this trip, Woman asked, "Really? How did you hear about this retreat?"

"I go to the yoga studio in Greenwich, but I live in Stamford." Stamford is the neighboring town to Greenwich but a significantly less wealthy town.

Woman, looking me up and down like I was an alien, apparently one of the single, childless, and not obscenely wealthy variety, then turned to talk to the other women and completely ignored me.

After several of these abrupt "conversations," I gave up and decided to just enjoy the view out the window. Maybe these women would be friendlier after the jet lag wore off? That said, they seemed to be quite chatty with each other, so I inadvertently and indirectly learned a lot about them and how different I was turning out to be from the rest of the group. Here's a small list of differences I compiled on the way to Umbria:

1. I am husband-free.

2. I am child-free.

3. I don't live in Greenwich.

4. I had never heard of the private school their kids all went to.

5. I have a paying job and pay my own bills.

6. I am capable of engaging in conversation on topics other than children I don't know and private schools I have never heard of in Greenwich.

Clearly, my efforts at not being judgmental weren't exactly succeeding. And I should also note that not all of the women met all of the above criteria. One didn't have kids, and three had paying jobs—two of whom were the yoga instructors for the group. But overall, this was a whole different league of people than I typically interact with in my real life. Greenwich, Connecticut, has some of the best public schools in the US and these women sent their kids to private elementary schools that cost about as much per year as a typical American university. Also, the median home price in Greenwich is well over one million dollars, so not exactly an affordable place to live. Yet almost none of these women had paying jobs outside of the home. This was clearly a privileged group of women. Or rather, a group of women married to privilege.

I have an interesting relationship to privilege and wealth. I grew up in Connecticut, but in a part *The New York Times* refers to as "up-and-coming." My great-grandparents and one of my grandparents immigrated to the US from southern Italy in the early 1900s. They were poor and generally uneducated; only one of my grandparents earned a high school diploma, and that was later in life through general equivalency. But they worked hard in the factories to make a better life for their families. My parents' generation also worked hard and were slightly more educated, so my upbringing was solidly middle class.

Impressed with the premise of the American dream from a young age, I studied my way into Dartmouth and then Wharton, where I met people whose upbringing and lifestyles were straight out of the society pages. I often feel like I occupy an odd space where I can float back and forth between the middle class I grew up in and the more privileged world I have some access to now, seeing the opportunities and challenges on each side. In many ways, I feel like an outsider, not really fitting in with either group. It never occurred to me growing up that I could simply marry my way into privilege or wealth; it was always important to me to earn my way there. And it completely blew my mind that actual people really lived like this—dependent on men to sustain their lifestyle.

To be honest, their lives seemed lavish, but they didn't seem all that happy. There was constant competition among them. Who had traveled to the most exotic places, who shopped where, whose kids had done what, etc., etc., etc. It was exhausting trying to keep up with their efforts to keep up with the Joneses. The community around their kids' private school seemed myopic and insular at best, a real-life version of *The Stepford Wives* at worst. And many of their husbands didn't sound like great life partners. Stories were shared about men who only noticed their wives when they were gone or who were extremely critical of weights and general appearances. In many cases, these men sounded more like keepers than partners—keepers for the kept. In general, the group ignored me, except when they offered tips on how to find a rich older man to "take me to amazing places," which was puzzling, since I actively take myself to amazing places already. Every conversation we had, I felt like they were talking down to me. In many ways, these women and their lifestyle were more foreign to me than the actual foreign country we were in.

And I found myself feeling really conflicted. On one hand, I realized I was envious of them. Their lives seemed so easy to me. Nannies took care of their kids; they were financially secure and didn't have to work for it; someone addressed all of their needs. They had husbands and families and money to protect them. In contrast, I spend so much of my time seeking financial security and trying to do work that I can be passionate about that also supports me. My financial security is rooted in what I can accomplish with my own talents and efforts: If I don't earn enough or save enough, no rich parents or husband will fund me. It's all on me to secure my present and my future, and I feel the weight of that responsibility every day.

At the same time, unlike these women, I don't answer to anyone and would hate to be dependent on someone else. I can do whatever I want in life, so long as it doesn't get me arrested or fired. If I, for example, feel like going to Italy on a whim and can convince my boss to approve it, I can just go. I have no kids to secure or husband to entertain, which is pretty empowering. And I can buy anything I feel like buying—subject to the constraints of my bank account, of course—without asking anyone for permission. I can pick up and move to another country. My options and choices in life are limited only by my capacity to dream and/or fund them. I don't have to worry about a man leaving me and torpedoing my lifestyle options.

So, it was an emotional week for me, spending time with women who generally weren't very nice to me, and for whom I felt a mix of envy, disdain, and pity. There were a few bright spots: the night we had a wine tasting that made everyone a bit friendlier, meeting the handsome olive farmer and learning about how olive oil is made (I swear I was interested in learning about olives!), the trip to Florence and art-historian-guided tour of the Uffizi. But overall, it was not the relaxing week I had been hoping for.

In this conflicted emotional space, I found myself on a minibus, in the middle seat of the back row, between two of the kept women, on our way to Assisi. Even though I was sitting between them, they were having a conversation over my head like I wasn't even there. While this may seem abnormal, being spoken over was such a frequent occurrence during this week that I was starting to question if I had inadvertently acquired an invisibility cloak.

One of the women said her husband would be traveling the night of her children's private school's fundraising gala, and she didn't want to go alone.

"Is there a singles table?" asked the lady to my left, over my head, to the lady on my right. "Could you sit there?"

"I think there is one, but I don't think I'd be comfortable sitting there," responded Lady on My Right.

Lady to My Left responded quite seriously, "Well, of course not, good point. Who wants to sit with the lonely-hearts club? Totally pathetic people."

These women knew I was single, and I completely couldn't believe that Lady to My Left had just labeled all single people as "pathetic" while sitting right next to me and literally talking over my head to Lady on My Right.

Lady to My Left, a.k.a., Mean Lady, continued, "You can't sit with all the pathetic, single women. Are you sure you can't convince your husband to join you? If not, just skip it. That's safer."

I'm sorry, safer? What on earth were the single people going to do to her? I shot her a confused look as I tried to fight back tears. I mean, obviously these women looked down on me for being single, but to effectively call me pathetic to my face seemed unnecessarily cruel.

Mean Lady finally acknowledged me. "I wasn't talking about you, of course!" she said, unconvincingly.

Holding back tears, I managed to say, "You're just saying what everyone thinks anyway," and looked straight ahead. Luckily, we arrived in Assisi a few minutes later. I think Mean Lady and Lady on My Right continued to talk, but I was too numb to listen.

Once we got off the bus, I did what any sensitive, thirty-something woman would do when in Italy after having very hurtful things said to her: I went to a cafe, ordered two cannoli and a double espresso, and texted my mother.

Me: "I'm in Assisi right now. It's beautiful here. But I'm a little upset. One of the women on my trip said something really thoughtless and hurtful today, and I can't seem to get it out of my head."

I filled my mom in on all the lurid details of the physically over-my-head conversation between Mean Lady and Lady on My Right.

Me: "So, I looked at Mean Lady like WTF and she's like, 'I'm not saying you're pathetic, of course,' but she was looking at me like, 'Of course, you are pathetic.'"

Me: "I guess I know married women look down on me, but no one has ever said that to my face before. I mean, she said being single is pathetic."

Me: "Do you think she was intentionally being mean? Maybe it's just so obvious in her mind that single women are pathetic that she didn't even realize what she was saying?"

Me: "Anyway, I need to stop thinking about this."

Me: "What do you think?"

Yes, I seriously sent a series of increasingly lame texts in a row to my mother. Luckily, my stereotypical Italian mom is the perfect person to reach out to while having an emotional meltdown that even cannoli in a charming Italian town can't fix. "Feisty" would be an appropriate, if dramatically understated, description of her. She is basically the human Italian American version of the Energizer Bunny. She never sleeps, seems to be constantly cooking delicious things, which she will force you to eat in increasingly less subtle ways, and is the greatest defender of her children imaginable. Seriously, I could commit murder and my mother would find some way to justify this behavior because there is no possible way her child could just be wrong. So, this desperate text message outreach was actually the perfect thing to do. I had been crossed and my mom would fix it, even from across the pond. Not surprisingly, my mom texted me back almost immediately.

Mom: "When people say things like that, it's mostly because they are jealous."

Me: "Why would they be jealous of someone they think is pathetic? I can't wait for this trip to end. I just want to avoid them all. This really hurts!"

Mom: "They are jealous of the freedom you have. I would brag about all the fun things you do just to rub it in. Don't stop doing things because of them. Then stupid people like that win. These ladies are pathetic if they can only talk about their kids."

I thought about this for a few minutes and then realized I didn't have much to lose by trying it. These women looked down on me. Many of them were way snootier than I could ever possibly dream of being. Why not test my mother's theory? Who cared if they thought I was a jerk?

As luck would have it, an opportunity presented itself that night at dinner. I was sitting near the end of the community table not too far from Mean Lady, within hearing distance. She was talking to another woman about how great this trip had been and how she was disappointed to be going home so soon. I decided to jump in.

"I know what you mean. I figured I would be sad to leave, so that's why I planned ahead to extend my trip. After this,

I'm off to Naples and the Amalfi Coast. It's been such a busy travel year for me! I mean, I was in London and Israel for work, and in Greece twice, and now I'm here! And I'm off to London for my birthday in November, too!"

I'm not kidding; I had barely finished this highly obnoxious discourse before Mean Lady got up and left the table. Mom was totally right.

* * *

I was the last of the group to leave the farm. I watched all the kept women board their shuttle bus with their absurd amounts of luggage, blindly following each other and their shallow expectations. I somehow managed to almost be the "bigger person," giving hugs and well-wishes and actually meaning them, but I was honestly thrilled to see their bus drive away down the long gravel road. I was surprised to find that I felt bad for them and also really grateful for our time together. Thanks to them, I'd seen a model of what I never wanted to be—a kept woman. I'd been forced to really consider my value as a human, and to realize that the act of making babies didn't make these women more valuable than me by default. Having a better understanding of the motivations behind their bad behavior strangely triggered a little empathy, and I realized these types of comments wouldn't get under my skin in the future. My life might be unconventional, but I chose it. I might have less money, but what I had, I earned myself and I owed nothing to no one. They were trapped, but I was free.

Soon, my taxi arrived. I watched out the window as we drove away from the rustic farmhouse that had been my home for the week, and through the beautiful winding, steep countryside of Umbria until we arrived at the Cortona train station. Sitting alone on a bench, eating Italian chocolates and listening to the tourists and other travelers around me as I waited for my train to Naples, I felt independent and invigorated. Nothing is better than exploring the world on your own terms.

The Revelation of Naples

B oth of my parents' families came from Italy, and I grew
up 100 percent Italian. We were the stereotypical Italian American family. We ate lots of pasta with "gravy," did
the traditional Sunday mid-afternoon "dinner" with family
and people we called aunts and uncles who were not actually related and shouted at each other across dinner tables
whether we were happy or angry. In fact, love was expressed
through food and shouted conversations over meals. I don't
remember ever leaving my grandparents' house without a
huge container of homemade gnocchi, eggplant parmesan,
fried peppers, or something from the garden to take home.

We also Italianized American traditions. In my family,
Thanksgiving turkey stuffing was made with ground sausage,
ground beef, parmesan cheese, eggs, and a few breadcrumbs
to bind it all together; we effectively stuffed our turkey with
a giant meatball. I didn't know until I went to college that
stuffing is usually not meatball based. For Easter, we ate ham
because that's what Americans do, and lasagna because you
can't have Sunday dinner without something requiring gravy.

Curious if I was truly as Italian as it seemed, I decided
to do DNA testing, which included a chart showing where

my ancestors had lived for the past three hundred years. I think the idea is to show that we all come from a lot of places. Except I don't. My chart is a bullseye around Naples, with tiny circles expanding out within southern Italy. I couldn't be more "Neapolitan" if I tried.

The first time I went to Italy, I backpacked after my study abroad in London and visited Venice, Florence, and Rome. On later trips, I visited Milan and the Lake Como region. All of these central and northern Italian areas were lovely, but I was always a bit puzzled by the experience. I didn't really feel a connection to the "mother land," as it were. The food was different. I did not grow up eating risotto, and where were all the red sauces and cheese? The language sounded crisper and more measured than what I grew up listening to, and the people were a lot taller and blonder than my family. It was beautiful, but it all felt foreign. I felt much more at home in Greece, especially the island of Santorini, than I did in Italy. It seemed odd to me that I could grow up so immersed in Italian American culture and find no personal connection with Italy. Given that my family is from the Naples area, I decided I needed to go south to see if that felt any more familiar. When I made plans to join the yoga retreat in Umbria, I tacked on a few days at the end to see Naples and find out if I felt connected to the country of my ancestors or not.

Exactly everyone I knew tried to talk me out of going to Naples on my own:

"It's dangerous."

"It's dirty."

"There's nothing to see there."

While I knew Naples had a bad reputation, this wasn't about seeing it as a tourist; I was on a mission to understand my roots. By that time, my grandparents and great aunts and uncles had all passed away, and I was yearning for a deeper understanding of their lives and, by transference, my own. I was also feeling adrift in the post-divorce world and really wanted to feel connected and rooted somewhere.

I was really close to my husband's family. I called his parents Mom and Dad, frequently called on them both for advice, and watched his brothers grow up. His youngest brother was only five when we started dating, and he had become my constant companion and sidekick over the years. But that all ended abruptly when we split. In many ways, losing my husband's family hurt more than losing him; a whole area of connection in my life was severed. With one less family to call my own, it seemed even more important to truly understand the one I had left and to learn more about myself in the process.

But when the yoga retreat ended, and it was time to finally see Naples, I felt conflicted. On one hand, I was thrilled to leave the largely unpleasant group of yoga retreaters and be back on my own again, a way of traveling I had grown to love in recent years. On the other hand, I was anxious, wondering if Naples would be as bad as people had said and worrying that I still might not feel any connection to my family. I have a very clear memory of sitting on a bench at the Cortona train station, eating *Baci Perugina* chocolates while contemplating the journey ahead.

As soon as I got off the train and into the central station in Naples, I felt an intense energy that seemed somehow familiar. It was loud and crazy and overwhelming, and I felt surprisingly invigorated as I navigated my way through the city's subway system to the stop closest to my boutique hotel. The hotel was incredibly quirky, but somehow absolutely perfect. Tucked into a strange alley near a large, slightly run-down square, the hotel occupied the top floors of an office building. The entrance was sort of an enclosed wooden frame around a parking lot with no cars that led directly to a glass-walled elevator. It felt kind of like when Harry Potter enters the Ministry of Magic through the telephone booth "visitors' entrance"—weird, but it sort of made sense in context.

And my room was probably one of my favorite rooms I've ever stayed in. It was also, quite possibly, the tiniest. To be fair, the size of the room was clear when I booked it. It was described as perfect for single travelers with light luggage. The entrance was a pocket door because the room was too small for the door to swing, the room held a twin-sized bed, and I'm pretty sure I could touch both walls with my arms extended the width of the room. That said, it was very modern, with high-end finishes and a disproportionately large all-marble bathroom. The hotel also boasted a rooftop terrace with panoramic views of Naples and Mount Vesuvius. I loved it.

I dropped my luggage in my room—or rather, squeezed it between the bed and the wall—and visited the concierge desk for recommendations. A lovely young woman named Anna was there to help. I explained that my family was from the Naples area, and I was looking to have a really traditional experience. While I'm sure she must hear this often—so many Americans have Italian roots—she seemed thrilled to help me on my mission and immediately started talking about food. I really liked her.

"Traditional food, let me think," she said. "On Sundays, we eat the traditional meal in the middle of the afternoon. And the most traditional food is something we call *Genovese*. Have you heard of this? A few restaurants nearby are famous for this."

I nearly passed out. Of course, the Sunday meal was in the middle of the afternoon. My family has done this every weekend since I can remember. That wasn't what surprised me. The part that got me was the *Genovese*, pronounced properly. My family called it "geno-ways;" Anna was actually pronouncing all the vowels. My grandmother's version of pot roast, it's usually a less expensive cut of meat cooked for hours in water with onions and carrots and white wine, resulting in a rich, oniony sauce and the most tender meat you can imagine. I grew up eating this at home but had never seen it on a menu and was floored to hear that several restaurants were famous for this.

"Yes, I know *Genovese*! I love *Genovese*!" I said, very excitedly. Except, for once, my over-excited-ness didn't seem to cause alarm. My new friend got equally excited.

"Well, then, you must have it!" she said, just as excitedly. And then she pulled out a map and noted every restaurant she liked, what traditional foods they were famous for, and the best time to go to each of them. We continued to chat enthusiastically for a while about my family and the specific villages where they grew up, as well as Anna's family and the things she liked and didn't like about Naples. She confided that a lot of tourists didn't like Naples and was hoping I would have a better time. She also felt strongly that I should have brought my mother with me to experience the city, which seemed to be a common theme in Italy. It should also be noted that this entire conversation took about thirty seconds, given that we were talking as if we'd both consumed our weight in espresso. To me, it felt oddly familiar—this manner of enthusiastic conversation, the warmth and energy I could feel from Anna as we spoke. I had a good feeling about this trip.

Promising to report my experience to Anna when I returned, I headed out to explore the city. Immediately, Naples felt like home to me. Walking through the busy streets filled with fiery, fast-talking people whose hands moved as quickly as they spoke, it was hard not to think of my family. And everywhere I looked, I saw the foods I grew up eating. I saw a man on the street roasting chestnuts like my grandfather used to do. I saw a giant poster in front of a bakery advertising *pasticciotto*, a cream-filled pastry that looks kind of like a cupcake covered with powdered sugar, that my other grandfather would always buy for special occasions. Another bakery was selling *struffoli*, marble-sized fried dough balls dressed with honey and sprinkles, that I used to make with my great aunt. Yet another had created a replica of Mount Vesuvius made of rum-soaked *babà*, my grandfather's favorite pastry.

Growing up, the Italian churches in my neighborhood hosted summer festivals where they served *pizza fritta*—basically fried dough like you'd expect to see at a state fair anywhere in the US, only topped with tomato sauce and parmesan cheese. Turns out this is a thing in Naples; street vendors sell it throughout the city. And then there's *ragu*: You can literally order a bowl of meat sauce and a huge hunk of bread as an appetizer. Even though I didn't speak much Italian at the time, I understood all the menus because these were the foods I'd been eating all my life but had never seen on a menu ever before.

I don't actually know why this was such a shock to me. Obviously, these recipes that my grandparents made had come from somewhere. I think it was just that I had spent my entire life having to explain the foods my family ate at home—it always felt like no one outside of my neighborhood had ever heard of them—so it was both strange and awesome to see those same foods out in public.

I spent the entire day eating, texting pictures of what I was eating along with goofy comments like "remember this?"

and "look familiar?" to my mother, and squealing with delight about basically everything and everyone I saw. Not only was I excited about the food, but I was also excited to see that my disproportionate enthusiasm did not seem out of place here. People in Naples were vibrant and full of life; it seemed that everyone was talking excitedly to everyone else. For the first time in Italy, I felt like I made sense here, like I should be speaking loud and furious Italian along with everyone else. Naples was quite simply a revelation. Sure, it was loud and dirty and urban—a very far cry from the rolling hills of Tuscany. But it was real, and for me, it was a connection to my family and heritage that I had never felt before in Italy, or really, ever.

Naples is famous for cameo jewelry, so the next day, I visited a shop to buy cameos for my mother and sister. Traveling around Italy, I've observed an interesting phenomenon. While shop workers there are almost always friendly and helpful, if you tell them you are buying a gift for your mother, they enter a whole new level of helpfulness hyperdrive and will do absolutely anything and everything to take care of you. I'm not sure why this happens—maybe because family is so important in Italy—but it's a remarkably consistent and adorable pattern. A jewelry shop owner in Bellagio turned her entire shop upside down for me on a quest for a specific ring my mother had admired on a friend. A pottery shop owner in Rome did the same thing when I mentioned that my mom really wanted ceramic figs. My mom really loves figs; amazingly, we found them. To avoid inconveniencing people, I actually try not to mention that I am buying gifts for my mom when I can avoid it. In this case, I told the owner of the shop that I was looking for two or three cameos as gifts. She asked me who they were for, and I didn't want to lie, so I reluctantly explained that I wanted to buy one each for my mom and my sister, and maybe one for myself, too. As expected, her face lit up.

"Your mother and your sister?" she asked me enthusiastically. "That is so sweet! You are such a good daughter! We will help you; it will be perfect!"

She recruited another shop worker to help, and together, they proceeded to pull out every cameo from the depths of the shop so I could fully understand my options. Tray after tray of beautiful cameos appeared and, after a really long time—it can take a while to look at every single cameo in a cameo shop in Naples—I finally decided on three beautiful pendants with floral designs. The largest and most expensive of the three was for my mom; the smallest and least expensive was for me. The shop owner was even more delighted when she understood that my mom's gift had taken priority.

As the other shop worker wrapped up my gifts, she announced, "You are part of our family now. We must have coffee together." This wasn't really a question, but I adore coffee and would never have turned it down in Italy, even if that had been an option.

It's important to note that the drinking of coffee in Italy is a ritual that must be executed precisely. Luckily, I have spent a lot of time loitering on the streets outside Italian coffee bars, so I knew the rules and was prepared for this impromptu test. First, if it's the afternoon, Italians don't drink *caffè latte* or *cappuccino*; beverages with milk are for mornings only. And espresso is the default form of coffee. As a result, when you go to a coffee bar, you just walk up to the cashier or barista, whoever is on the left-most side of the counter, and ask for *un caffè*. Then you pay, step immediately to the right and stay standing at the bar. A small glass of water appears, and you are supposed to drink that right away. Then the saucer for your espresso glass appears, and finally, the espresso itself. If there is a spoon in the espresso, it already has sugar in it and you should stir it with a few dramatic, yet seemingly careless flourishes (this looks so cool when real Italians do it; I'm sure I look like I have a strange twitch in my hand) and drink the espresso quickly—no more than a few sips. If the spoon is on the saucer, the espresso does not yet have sugar and you can add it if you wish. As soon as you drink the espresso, you leave.

The shop owner's assistant was still wrapping the three cameos when the coffee arrived; it was that fast. A beautiful tray holding three perfectly petite glasses of espresso along with three small water glasses was placed on the counter by the cash register. Elegant silver stirrers were inside each espresso. I was impressed by how quickly they had arrived, but even more so by how beautifully they were presented—and in glass cups. Takeout served in glassware is one of those things about Europe that always impresses me. We each drank our respective glass of water. Then, we each dramatically stirred with our silver stirrers and drank our espresso quickly. It was a beautiful bonding moment. I felt like Sophia Loren although I'm sure I didn't look even remotely that cool. At least I didn't slosh my espresso out of its perfect glass as I stirred it.

Coffee consumed and cameos wrapped and purchased, it was time to say goodbye. Just as I was leaving, the shop owner presented me with a tiny charm, a gift so I would always remember my time in Naples. Made of bright red coral attached to a silver bale, the charm looked like a delicate chili pepper. I recognized it right away: It was a *cornicello*, or little horn, a traditional good luck amulet popular in southern Italy that is worn to protect wearers from the evil eye curse. My grandfather always wore a gold *cornicello* pendant. I felt tears come to my eyes. In many ways, it felt like a gift from him, thanking me for visiting his hometown and trying to make this connection with my roots.

As I left the hotel in Naples and said goodbye to Anna, it was like saying goodbye to a long-lost sister. We hugged and I promised to visit again. She insisted that I bring my mom next time. On the taxi ride, the driver asked me what I thought of Naples.

"I loved it!" I said excitedly. "My family is from this area, and it was amazing to understand where they are from."

"We say here that people from Naples, they are like fire." He was smiling. "So, you must be very fiery."

When I think about this trip to Naples, I'm always struck by just how much of a revelation it was. At some level, I was expecting to leave with a better understanding of my family, and really hoping to discover a deeper connection with Italy. That was the revelation I was prepared to have, to the extent that anyone can be prepared in advance for a revelation. What surprised me was that these few days ended up being a too-brief journey of self-discovery. Suddenly, I made more sense to myself. I've spent my whole life trying to explain my intense enthusiasm and energy, only to find that being so fiery is part of my cultural heritage. Experiencing that firsthand, surrounded by an intensity that I innately understood, was an epiphany.

To me, life is a journey of phased discovery; you have to understand who you are to discover who you can be. I left Naples feeling, for the first time, truly grounded in who I was and ready to figure out where that would take me on the rest of the journey. I started to see myself as a complete person on my own and also rooted in a much bigger cultural heritage. And it was viscerally comforting to finally feel my roots in a place. After a lifetime of never quite feeling like I fit, I began to seriously consider that I might have just been living on the wrong continent.

The Empath and
the Sommelier

I don't generally consider myself to be a mind reader, but occasionally, it happens.

After my divorce, I discovered I was an empath. According to Judith Orloff, "the trademark of an empath is feeling and absorbing other people's emotions and/or physical symptoms because of their high sensitivities." This may sound kind of new-agey weird, and Google Dictionary would apparently agree, given that it defines an empath as "(chiefly in science fiction) a person with the paranormal ability to apprehend the mental or emotional state of another individual." To be clear, I don't think I have paranormal abilities although that seems like fun. I am super sensitive and absorb the emotions and, occasionally, the thoughts of others, which can be a blessing and a curse.

On the blessing side, it's generally clear to me who likes me and who doesn't and how people feel about whatever is happening wherever I am. This is a huge asset as a solo traveler. For example, I can make very smart decisions about which hot European waiters to go out with and which ones to avoid. On the downside, if I am in a room with cranky, anxious people, it's easy for me to become cranky and anxious—for example, my entire marriage. One thing I always find interesting is that it's much easier for me to pick up on others' thoughts and emotions the more strongly they are experiencing them. Also, I have very little control over when or where these insights may strike, like, for example, during a wine tasting in Napa.

My love of wine began in college when I took an extracurricular wine tasting class. At the time, my motivations were suspect at best. As the last of my friends to turn twenty-one, I was determined to do anything and everything I could to acknowledge my legal drinking status, including an absurd shopping spree at the local New Hampshire state liquor store that left me with a lifetime supply of Frangelico and Goldschläger because I was enamored of their pretty bottles. On the plus side, I created a fantastic concoction affectionately named the Merry Monk —hot cocoa, Frangelico, and Bailey's—in an effort to deplete my inventory. Also, it turns out that Goldschläger, prosecco, and apple cider make a killer punch. Anyway, despite my questionable motivations, I developed a passion for wine that continues to this day and actually learned a lot of useful things in that class:

- A deep and abiding love of big, bold red wines, including California cabernet

- The proper way to swirl a glass of wine before tasting it without splashing it out of the glass, no matter how many glasses I have already consumed

- An appreciation of the weirdly wonderful and occasionally, illogical, words used to describe wine: "eggplant," "earthy," "jammy," "bramble," "wet stones," etc. I love the way these words capture both the feeling and the flavor of a wine; they somehow make a lot of sense and no sense at the same time. It's fabulous.

There's just nothing better than the way a nice sip of wine feels as it brushes against my lips at the end of a long day, somehow celebratory and calming at the same time. Somewhat unbelievably, my ex-husband had an intolerance to wine. His whole face turned bright red after just a few sips, and he was instantly exhausted. I believe this fact constitutes another, slightly-less-subtle-than-a-fire-but-still sign from the Universe that I shouldn't have married him. Anyway, my love of big, bold California reds and the fact that my ex-husband would never have been interested landed a trip to Napa Valley on my post-divorce bucket list.

On one beautiful, sunny day in Napa Valley, I booked a tour and tasting at a winery outside of St. Helena. I was really excited since this particular winery is famous for both its cabernet sauvignon and its stunning landscape. On the tour with me that day were eight other people: a wine club member and two of her friends, and a group of five people who seemed to be connected to each other through a restaurant business. I, of course, was traveling solo. The wine club woman was friendly and down to earth (as down to earth as anyone who belongs to a prestigious Napa Valley wine club can be), and her friends seemed to be people who liked wine and were happy to drink the good stuff. The other group was a different story.

An older man, maybe in his late fifties or early sixties, who struck me as a slightly smarmy cross between a Wall

Street executive and Rhett Butler, seemed to be the connector of this group. With him was the textbook definition of your worst banker stereotype—tall, loud, self-important. There was also a kind-eyed older man who seemed too genuine to be part of this group, and a couple from the South—think deep southern drawls and big hair.

The husband immediately identified himself to our extraordinarily handsome, blue-eyed tour guide as a sommelier. I was already one glass into my tasting and I have a low alcohol tolerance, so my brain was a bit fuzzy, but I definitely remember thinking that was bold. I'm a yoga instructor; I don't feel compelled to identify myself as such when I walk into a yoga class. But this guy wanted us to know he was the wine expert in the group.

So, the nine of us headed over to the on-site mansion where we would do the official tasting with Blue Eyes. We were seated at a long wooden table in the dining room of the mansion, complete with stained-glass windows and a panoramic view of the pool and vineyards in the distance. It was incredible. I was at the center of the table, the wine club trio to my left and the group of five across and to the right. Despite the fact that we were drinking a lot of wine and wine usually makes people friendlier, or at least more talkative, I was having trouble making any inroads with this group. I had decided to just settle in and enjoy the amazing wines and blurry brain in peaceful solitude when Blue Eyes announced that he was going to challenge the sommelier. He was going to let us try a wine from the vineyard's "library" (i.e., a really old wine) and we were to guess the vintage (year) of the wine. The group was super excited; older wines like these are really expensive and really rare, so this was a treat for us.

Blue Eyes walked around the table, pouring each of us a sample of this mystery wine, careful to cover the label year with his pouring hand. I expertly swirled my glass (no spilling!) and inhaled deeply to smell what I was sure would be a delightful fragrance. Not so much. I got a whiff of dill with a subtle hint of feet. The rest of the table didn't seem horrified, so I braved the dill-feet and took a sip. It tasted better than it smelled, but it was most definitely not my cup of tea (wine?). I became aware of the absolute delight of the others around the table. They seemed to adore this wine and rhapsodized eloquently about its many qualities, using words like "soft" and "balanced." Blue Eyes asked me what I thought of the wine. In my efforts not to mention dill or feet, I said something extremely incoherent about the complexity of wines as they age. It was so lame that it seemed like even Smarmy Rhett Butler felt bad for me. The sommelier looked uncomfortably away from me and my ignorant comment.

And then something very clear popped into my head: 1979. The conversation continued around me with the table all avoiding me, and all I could think was 1979, 1979, 1979. Then Blue Eyes asked us to go around the table and guess the vintage. He started with the banker. I don't remember exactly what he guessed because inside my head was shouting, "1979!" And then I noticed that the sommelier, who would be the last to guess, was furiously writing what looked like equations on a sheet of paper. My math major brain was alternating between two thought spaces:

1. How are there equations in wine? Why would there be equations in wine? Can you solve an equation to get to a vintage? What would the other variables be? I really, really like equations.

2. 1979!

Blue Eyes turned to me. I was vaguely aware that everyone else had guessed a year in the mid-'80s to early '90s. I decided to go with 1979, so I could get back to thinking about wine equations. The entire table looked at me like I had just admitted to being a crack head who prefers beer to wine. Smarmy Rhett Butler couldn't contain himself.

"1979? That wine would be worth a fortune! Can you imagine, pouring wine from 1979 on a tour?"

The entire group laughed; the sommelier's wife and the genuine older man looked at me with closed-lip half smiles, suggesting their deep sympathy for my philistine-ness.

Then the sommelier guessed, "Based on the soft tannins and [blah, blah, blah], I would put this between 1983 and 1985." Everyone at the table nodded confidently, except me; I was trying to decipher his equations.

Blue Eyes prepared for the dramatic reveal. He seemed very amused, trying really hard not to laugh. "One of you was right!"

Everyone looked admiringly at the sommelier, assuming he had guessed correctly. He acknowledged his new fans with a wry smile and that head tilt really good-looking men make when adoring women swoon at them.

After a long pause, Blue Eyes finally spoke. "The vintage is . . . 1979!"

Silence.

Shock.

Total, complete shocked silence around the table.

It was awesome.

Smarmy Rhett Butler's jaw was actually on the table. Slowly, he returned it to its proper place on his face and started to applaud. The rest of the group joined him.

"How did you know it was 1979? That's amazing! What a refined palate you must have!"

Blue Eyes presented me with the 1979 bottle, with a bit left to drink; I graciously offered the remaining wine to the group. I still thought it smelled like dill with a hint of feet. On the walk back to the vineyard's entrance, Smarmy caught up with me, now very curious to know more about me. What other wineries did I like? Did I have any recommendations for him? How had I developed such a refined taste for wine?

Part of me felt bad about allowing him to think I was a secret wine expert, as opposed to a highly attuned empath. But then, a bigger part of me didn't feel very bad at all. And really, I had Blue Eyes to thank. He must have really been thinking hard about 1979 for it to appear so clearly in my befuddled brain like that. And did I mention how handsome he was?

The empty 1979 Cabernet bottle, fitted with a candelabra, sits on the top of my bookshelf at home, a constant reminder that empaths should never be underestimated.

Meet-Cute Meltdown

———

A really delightful concept in movies is called the "meet-cute." Described specifically in the adorable 2006 romantic comedy, *The Holiday*, a "meet-cute" is defined by the Merriam-Webster dictionary online edition as "a cute, charming, or amusing first encounter between romantic partners." As the character Arthur (Eli Wallach) says to Iris (Kate Winslet), "Say a man and a woman both need something to sleep in, and they both go to the same men's pajama department. And the man says to the salesman, 'I just need bottoms.' The woman says, 'I just need a top.' They look at each other, and that's the meet-cute." Meet-cutes can happen in a variety of places, including port wine lodges in Portugal.

I decided to go to Portugal after reading many articles about the best and cheapest places for Americans to retire abroad. As a single person, I think it's important to plan ahead for retirement so I don't have to worry about ending up destitute like Grizabella from the musical *Cats*, less any ability to sing through the pain. After scrolling through pages of places that seemed both unsafe and lacking medical services (perhaps they were "cheap" because my retirement would be shortened due to early death?), I discovered a location that sounded not totally insane—Carvoeiro, in the Algarve region of Portugal. On the southern coast of Portugal, Carvoeiro boasted dramatic cliffs with ocean views, a mild climate, fresh seafood, warm and friendly people, a low cost of living, and easy access to the rest of Europe.

My original plan was to visit Carvoeiro and Lisbon, the capital city, but a last-minute hotel issue forced me to adjust my itinerary to start the trip in the northern city of Porto. Porto is famous for port wines, which I love. They are thick, sweet, fortified wines, typically consumed with desserts, and positively luscious to drink. Plus, it feels so fancy to drink port. Every time I drink it, I feel like I should be wearing a navy-blue velvet smoking jacket while sitting on a Pottery Barn dark brown leather club chair with just enough wear in the arms to show some character, in a room with floor-to-ceiling bookshelves and one of those cool ladders that slides around so you can access the top-shelf books while commenting on the news of the day in a proper British accent. It's kind of like a cross between Hugh Hefner and Winston Churchill, minus the naked women, cigars, and mumbling.

Upon arriving in Porto, I realized I hadn't made any wine-tasting plans. I asked the concierge for recommendations, and he booked an appointment for me the next day at his favorite place, which included a tour of the property as well as a tasting. I spent the rest of my first day wandering around Porto's charming city center, discovering an ornate bookstore with a swirling red staircase that is falsely rumored to have inspired J.K. Rowling when she was writing the Harry Potter series.

I awoke the next day to steady rain but still decided to take the thirty-five-minute walk to the winery. At first, the walk was lovely despite the rain—strolling along old, windy streets with artisan shops and bakeries, on my way to the Douro

River. There, I crossed a beautiful metal bridge designed by Eiffel (yes, that one). It was, however, hard to appreciate how beautiful it was because its structure was downright slick in the rain, and I was stepping very carefully to avoid falling and sliding off the bridge. Once I crossed the bridge and kissed the firm ground beneath me, Google Maps sent me on a crazy walking route that seemed to somehow be entirely uphill. Frazzled and frizzy, I arrived at the winery and waited behind a large group of French tourists who were blocking the entire check-in area, so I was now late for my scheduled tour.

A handsome man with very kind eyes sensed my plight and asked me if I needed help. He checked me in and walked me to the room where the rest of my tour group was watching a video about the making of port. "You're just a few minutes behind, so don't worry," he assured me kindly. I liked him immediately. After the video, the same handsome man gathered us all together; he was my group's tour guide.

It obviously occurred to me that my tour guide was extremely handsome; I recall consciously considering if I should try to ask a great wine question to get his attention—this is my nerdy idea of flirting—but decided against it. I was in Portugal to relax, not impress boys, which is pretty much the opposite of relaxing. So, I quietly enjoyed learning about the history and making of port from this handsome and knowledgeable guide, confident in my decision to not flirt. At the end of the tour, Handsome Tour Guide brought us into the tasting room, where it took nearly every ounce of my self-control to keep from squealing with glee.

The tasting room was basically straight out of my imagined port-drinking world. It was a big room, filled with dark brown leather club chairs surrounding rich mahogany tables. Floor-to-ceiling bookshelves lined the walls, filled with pretentious-looking books with titles like *Port: A History*, or simply, *Wine*. Nestled into cubbies throughout the room were portraits of the company's founders and reserve bottles of aging port. I could even hear British accents, thanks to a lovely British couple on my tour. The only thing missing was the navy velvet smoking jacket; had one been offered to me, I probably would have cried. It was perfect. I took a seat in my designated club chair and settled in for the tasting, positively delighted with the Universe in that specific moment.

I brought myself back to reality to listen to Handsome Tour Guide's explanation of the wines we would be tasting. He worked his way around the room, chatting with each group on the tour and answering any questions that they had about the wines. Eventually, he made it to my table. We discussed the wines for quite a while. It turned out that we had very similar interest in and taste for wines. Then, our conversation turned to my plans while in Portugal. I told him I would be heading to Lisbon for a few days and then to the southern coast.

"That's interesting," he said. "I'm actually moving to the southern coast in a few days. It's beautiful there. What part will you visit?"

"I'm going to a town named Carvoeiro," I said. He looked confused. "I might not be pronouncing it right?" Turns out I was not. It is pronounced "Carve-WHERE-o" and I was saying something more like "CARV-eee-air-o." So, once we corrected this, he was like, "Wait, you're going to Carvoeiro? My new job is in Carvoeiro! And that's actually not a big town. It's so funny that you are going there, too!"

I was slightly surprised, but it didn't seem crazy to me, given that I was currently drinking delicious wine in my port dream room while chatting up an insanely handsome man I had previously decided not to flirt with.

"I'm starting a job as a sommelier at a new resort there; it's called Tivoli," he said.

"Did you say Tivoli? Seriously? That's where I'm staying!"

Now I was surprised because that was just crazy. He was moving to work at the same hotel I was going to? We compared dates and realized that he would arrive in Carvoeiro on my last day there. Over several more glasses of wine, we continued to chat—about the wine, Portugal, things I should do on my trip, his new job and excitement about the move, how we'd both lived in London before—and then exchanged numbers with the intention of connecting in person before I left Portugal. It was insane.

By this time, I was also a bit drunk. I do not typically drink multiple glasses of fortified wine in the middle of the day, and upon standing, I realized why this was a bad idea. I attempted to walk off the alcohol-induced haze in the lodge's shop, which seemed to help my brain if not my wallet. Eventually, I made my way outside for the descent into town, pleased with my day so far. I exited from a different door than I had entered and was a bit disoriented, so I picked a direction and started walking, thinking that I'd figure it out eventually. As luck would have it, I ran into Handsome Tour Guide (now, Handsome Sommelier) in the parking lot as he was getting out of a car.

Ducking under my umbrella, he asked, "Do you need some help?" He looked amused. I wasn't sure why.

"I'm just going to walk back to town," I said, trying to sound like I knew where I was going and was also totally sober.

"Ah, you want to be going that way," he said, pointing in the exact opposite direction. "I wish I could drive you myself, but I have to get back inside." He looked almost wistful and quite concerned for my well-being. It was lovely. "It was such a beautiful coincidence meeting you today."

And then I realized, this was beyond coincidence; this was a real-life meet-cute! I wasn't originally planning to visit Porto and I hadn't chosen the winery or the tour time. If any of these things had gone differently, we wouldn't have met. And then, not only was I going to the exact same town as he was for his new job, I was also going to the exact same hotel. By the time I arrived in Lisbon, we had exchanged a few texts and made plans to meet for dinner the following Saturday, the last night of my trip and Handsome Sommelier's first night in Carvoeiro. Oh, and Handsome Sommelier now had an actual name, Luis.

I forced myself to redirect my attention to the rest of my trip instead of daydreaming about the Saturday date, which was not easy given the excessive adorable-ness of the whole situation. After a few delightful days in Lisbon, I took the train south to the Algarve. Seeing this area was the whole reason for my trip. Was this a place where I could see myself retiring someday? As excited as I was to see it, I was also terrified because I had decided to rent a car to enable this exploration, my first ever international car rental. This was worrisome to me for several reasons:

1. I am not a great driver in my own car in my own country, where I theoretically know and understand the rules of the road and can read street signs.

2. I have a terrible sense of direction and wasn't sure how GPS would work abroad.

3. I would be driving on unfamiliar roads alone in a country where I don't speak the language and wasn't sure what to do in case of emergency (beyond crying).

With significant trepidation, I met the rental car company representative at my hotel, where he was dropping the car off to me. I signed a bunch of papers and he showed me the car—a tiny, charcoal grey Opel Corsa. I had never heard of either the car or the brand but was reassured by how cute it was. He explained how everything worked and it all made sense until he said, "Let me make sure you know how to park this car. It doesn't have a 'P.'"

"I'm sorry?" I asked. "What do you mean it doesn't have a 'P'?" I should mention that I have never, in my entire life, driven a car that was not automatic. My car at home has a "P" button that I push to park it.

"'P' for 'Park,'" he said. That part, I understood. "You need to put the car into neutral and pull up the brake to park it."

"The emergency brake?" I asked.

"The parking brake," he said.

"Oh, right. Park with the parking brake. Makes sense!" I said with feigned enthusiasm. Didn't someone tell me once that I should only use "neutral" if my car was being towed?

He left me with the car, and I went back to my room to reconsider my plan. Previously, I had been worried about *driving* my rental car in a foreign country. Now I was also worried about *parking* it.

Never one to back down from a challenge, I decided to go all-in. I really wanted to go to Cape St. Vincent, at the southern "corner" of Portugal with panoramic views of the Atlantic Ocean. The problem: It was an hour and a half away from where I was at that moment. I decided to go for it anyway. What better way to conquer my fear of driving in a foreign country than driving a really long distance in a car I wasn't sure I could drive or park in a foreign country? I think this is like exposure therapy or something.

Although initially harrowing, the drive was ultimately a success. The death grip I had on my phone, which was serving as GPS, slowly loosened as I drove. I guess it was good that I didn't know southern Portugal had roundabouts every five feet before I set out on my journey, but the plus side is that I can now cross both "international car rental" and "roundabouts" off my list of driving-related fears. When you drive through at least one hundred roundabouts, you become quite desensitized to them.

Cape St. Vincent was absolutely stunning. I will never forget the sheer beauty of that drive. As I drove along the road, suddenly it just opened up to green grass, steep limestone cliffs, and ocean in every direction, as far as the eye could see. And, in the distance, a red lighthouse sat at that exact point where ocean and land met. It felt like I was part of the landscape; I was so transfixed that I completely forgot my parking fears. I just wanted to get out of that car and frolic under the sun along the southern edge of Europe.

Empowered by the freedom of having my own car, I decided to take myself to several well-recommended restaurants in the area that were too far to reach by foot. One in particular looked awesome. Michelin starred, it promised a feast for the senses and a cultural experience of Portugal through food. Incredibly excited, I hit the road in my tiny car, ready for a culinary adventure. I'm kind of a foodie, in a weird way. Even though I don't enjoy cooking and am not very good at it (possibly related), I love to eat, have worked in the food industry for the past decade, and enjoy learning about local culture through food.

I'm also generally at ease eating by myself. It can be intimidating at first. There's this feeling that everyone around you is staring at you and wondering why you are alone. Work travel helped to take the edge off of this because it made my solo dining easy to explain; it's common for business people to travel alone for work. Eventually, I realized that other diners generally aren't paying much attention to me, whether I'm alone or not. And, since I love food so much, it can actually be quite nice to enjoy a meal and be fully engaged in that experience without having to talk to anyone. And to order whatever I want without compromising or feeling awkward (some days are two dessert kinds of days). I used to play with my phone or write in my journal to keep myself busy, but I've come to a place where I enjoy quietly savoring a meal in peace without any distractions.

As long as I don't get seated at the bar. I hate trying to enjoy my meal calmly while staring at someone I don't know who is working and not eating. That's awkward. Do I try to talk to this stranger? Or do I look down and eat as fast as possible? Those are the only options, really. I'll take a table by myself any day.

Arriving at the restaurant, I was immediately surprised by how small it was. It was a hexagonal room with an open floor plan and maybe ten well-spaced tables. One hexagonal wall housed the coolest wine cellar I have ever seen—enormous rounded rectangular glass doors with maple-colored wooden trim that made a soft whooshing sound when they slid open or closed. It was futuristic in a kind of 1960s way, which I think means it was very mod. Or Danish? I don't know, but it was a super cool design element in an otherwise minimalist space. I was seated at a table opposite the whooshing wine cellar doors, in clear view of the other nine tables. I definitely felt seen, and I felt the room's surprise at a single diner in such a fancy restaurant, so I wasn't exactly off to a great start. I decided to try the chef's tasting menu, which began with "snacks."

Quickly, the first "snack" arrived: a fake walnut atop a tray of real walnuts. I had no silverware or bread plate, and the waiter was standing in front of me with this tray of walnuts. I wasn't sure what to do. It occurred to me that this would be one situation where a dining partner could have been helpful. I picked up the fake walnut and prepared to take a bite. I had no idea what the fake walnut really was, or what would happen when I tried to bite it. Was I supposed to eat it whole? It seemed too big for that. I took a small bite, and it was delicious! A thin shell covering a blend of beets and goat cheese that could definitely be eaten in a few bites. Surely, silverware would arrive soon and food I recognized would appear.

Still no silverware, but the next snacks were crostini. I knew how to eat those, so that was good. And then a bread basket appeared with homemade bread and three butters blended with goat cheese, peppers and carrots, respectively. This would have been awesome, except that the butters were presented as balls, perched precariously on top of a rock-shaped piece of pottery. It reminded me of the clay "art" I made for my mom in elementary school, only this one was balancing three balls of butter. How exactly was I supposed to get the butter on the bread without dropping it on the table or, worse, flinging it across the restaurant? Now, I was getting frustrated. Eating alone is one thing, but trying to eat alone with a full staff of waiters and other diners watching you as you figure out how to not throw your food around a super fancy restaurant is just not fun at all. For the first time in ages, I really wished I was not alone.

And then I realized that spending a lot of money being cranky was not part of my travel plans. I decided that I didn't care if I spilled food or looked like a philistine. Who was I trying to impress? This food may be crazy, but maybe I could view the situation as an opportunity to play with my food and enjoy the wacky experience instead of being frustrated. It was a convenient thought because the final snack was quite impressive. A brandy snifter filled with not brandy was placed in front of me, along with what looked like a nest made of shredded phyllo with a small quail egg inside. What on earth was I supposed to do with this? I asked the waiter.

Gesturing toward the brandy snifter, he said, "This is consommé with citrus ice. It is accompanying a quail egg nest."

Obviously.

"And how do you suggest I eat this?" I asked, trying really hard to remember that food is fun and I was enjoying the experience.

"In whichever order you would like," the waiter replied. "But be careful with the egg. It is soft-boiled."

I took a deep breath and dove in and did not end up dripping quail egg yolk or making a huge mess, much to my relief. It was really delicious, an amazing combination of flavors. Finally, silverware arrived, so at least I had utensils to puzzle through the rest of my meal. Most of the rest of the courses made sense to me. And the chef even came out to explain one of the courses that didn't, so I really did get to learn about local culture through food. By the time the wasabi caviar palate cleanser (seriously!) arrived, I had totally embraced the experience, asking assuredly ridiculous questions of the waiters and eating with gusto. I forgot about the other diners entirely.

At the end of the meal, one of the waiters appeared with a beautiful jewelry box and asked if I liked jewels. When the box was dramatically opened, it contained a stunning variety of chocolate truffles, filled with local flavors like port. I may have actually giggled out loud; it was just such an over-the-top way to cap this dining adventure.

I spent my last days in Portugal visiting beautiful beaches, sitting under the sun on soft sand, and admiring the clear water, amazing rock formations, and caves that this region is famous for. I was so relaxed, in fact, that I was surprised to find that it was 4:00 p.m. on Saturday and I hadn't heard from Luis about our planned dinner that night. I was now starting to consider the possibility that this trip wasn't going to end with the grand romantic fairy tale that had been dancing in my mind—holding hands while strolling along a stunning beach at sunset, sipping delightful Portuguese wines, laughing about the twists of fate that had brought us together. Sometimes, my imagination gets the best of me. This is what actually happened.

I considered just letting the situation go. If he didn't reach out, it wasn't meant to be. But I'm a little too Type A for that, so I texted him to see if he was still up for dinner. A few minutes later, he replied.

"Dear Sara, I am so sorry! I am visiting my sister and will not be back tonight to Carvoeiro. I'd love to see you on Sunday if you are free? If not, you must promise me that you will come back soon. :)"

This was obviously a rather abysmal departure from my fantasy scenario.

Disappointed, I texted back, "I am leaving at 6:15 tomorrow morning, so it will be too early to meet. I will definitely let you know if I make it back to Portugal!"

Almost immediately after sending this text, I irrationally concluded that it was snarky, so I sent another.

"I hope you're having a great visit with your sister! I am sorry to leave so early tomorrow. It was so nice meeting you!"

His reply seemed decidedly less friendly.

"It was nice to meet you. I wish you a nice last day in Portugal."

I would love to report that I learned a valuable lesson in expectations management from this experience (i.e., high expectations dashed are worse than low expectations met, even if the outcome is exactly the same). Unfortunately, I decided to take myself to the local wine bar. After a few glasses of wine, it was clear to me that I needed to send Luis another text, and I came up with this gem:

"Thank you for teaching me so much about port! You are such a great teacher!"

As if this text wasn't lame enough, while attempting to send it, I accidentally *video called* him, immediately hung up, and still sent the text.

Um, yeah.

Not surprisingly, I never heard back from him but may have coined a new term in the process, the Modern Age opposite of the "meet-cute," the "text-ugly."

In Portugal, in addition to experiencing a beautiful country and culture that I can definitely envision living in someday, I conquered my fear of driving abroad, something that will no longer hold me back for future adventures. I found a way to turn solo dinner awkwardness into a joyful, memorable experience. I even took a chance on a real-life meet-cute. I embraced my independence through the excitement and the discomfort and put myself out there in ways I hadn't before.

And who knows? Maybe a few decades from now, sitting on the terrace of my retirement home in Carvoeiro, Luis and I will hold hands at sunset while drinking port in matching navy-blue smoking jackets, laughing about the ridiculous coincidences that brought us together.

Late Night Algarve

It was a crummy day in the Algarve, the southern coast of Portugal, largely of my own making. Although I was on vacation, I had spent the entire morning working and the early afternoon fighting with Wi-Fi to submit that work. The having-to-work part was not my fault. My narcissistic, workaholic (and, to make matters worse, wildly unapprecia-tive) boss was to blame for that. I was angry about having to work and even angrier that I couldn't stop being angry about having to work, a rather miserable and irrational vortex drawing me further and further away from the relaxation I sought. I found myself sitting by the pool in one of the most beautiful spots in the world, fuming. Needing to break the cycle, I decided to take a walk along the cliffs, and hopefully, not over them, *Thelma and Louise* style.

After about an hour of walking, I felt more like my non-furious self. I had to stay focused to avoid losing my footing on the steep surfaces, and the views were stunning. I watched the sun reflect off sheer limestone cliffs, carved erratically by the ocean, creating stripes of beige and white that gracefully flowed into the teal-colored water. Occa-sionally, I'd spot a hidden beach tucked under the cliffs, or a natural archway in the rocks leading to a secret cave. I finally felt the tension of the day leave my body as I wandered and watched.

And then my phone vibrated, and I instantly felt my blood boil. Assuming my boss was texting, I pulled my phone out of my pocket, ready to explode. Much to my shock and delight, it was definitely not my boss; it was Luis, the handsome sommelier I had met on a previous trip to Portugal. A few days earlier, I had texted him to let him know I was returning but hadn't expected to hear back given the awkward ending of my last visit. Unexpectedly, he wrote that he was working at a beach club and restaurant a forty-five minutes' drive away. Did I want to stop by that night?

Perhaps more shocking than this invitation was that I was so mired in my intense cranky petulance that I actually considered saying no. Gratefully, logic returned. The man is stunning. And seemed to *not be a jerk*. I didn't actually think that was possible, but it seemed like a hypothesis worth validating! Decision made, I made fast work of the return hike, put on my cutest dress, and drove out to meet the handsome sommelier.

Arriving at the beach club, I saw an absolute vision standing atop an elegant white staircase at the entrance—tanned hands posed casually on the top railing, leading to a crisp white shirt and formal vest. Thick, dark hair and one of the most handsome faces I had ever seen. The man was even more gorgeous than I remembered. And he seemed really excited to see me? Praying not to trip, I ascended the stairs on wobbly legs, trying to process the insane contrasts of my day. A few hours ago, I was hunched angrily over my computer, and now I was meeting this gorgeous man at a super fashionable beach club. Crazy.

When I successfully reached the top of the stairs, we did the two-cheek kiss thing and Luis exclaimed excitedly, "I really can't believe you're here! I'm so happy to see you!"

An aside: I totally don't get this. My "dating life" in the US is hypothetical at best. No handsome American sommeliers are waiting to see me when I return from my adventures. Yet, when I go to Europe, I seem to be a beacon for gorgeous, interesting European men. I'm not complaining; I'm honestly baffled. Here are my best guesses as to why this happens:

1. European men have extremely different taste than American men. This certainly holds true for fashion, and usually in a good way, with two notable exceptions: manpris (capri pants for men; gross) and speedos (way more gross).

2. Sara in Europe is way more appealing than Sara in America. This actually seems plausible, if alarming. In the US, I'm usually working and often angry about how much I'm working, or the work itself. So, I'm either at work physically or mentally, which doesn't leave much room for men. It seems slightly troubling that my "real" life repels others; I should come back to this.

So, back to the story. Luis took me on a tour of the beautiful club, a posh place with cabanas, a swim-up pool bar and recliner chairs in the pool that had bar service, as well as a full-service restaurant. He proudly showed me the wine list he designed for the restaurant. It really felt like we had known each other forever; the conversation flowed easily, and we kept finding more things to talk about. This was incredible because we only met once before, when he was my tour guide at a port wine "lodge" in Porto, Portugal, a few months earlier. During the conversation, he mentioned that he was cat-sitting for a friend. I couldn't resist probing further:

"You like cats?" I asked, attempting to sound like this wasn't a super important thing for me to know.

"Yes, of course. I like dogs, too, but cats are so interesting."

So, Handsome Sommelier also *liked cats*. This was seriously a Hallmark Channel movie. Was he also about to announce that he was secretly the prince of a heretofore unknown European country?

"Do you have any pets?" he asked.

"Just one cat," I said, doing my best to downplay my crazy cat-lady-ness and also hide my favorite giant cat ring that I happened to be wearing that night. It's actually subtler than it sounds, but still.

"Who watches your cat for you when you travel?" he asked. Was Handsome Sommelier confirming that I'm single?

"I have a pet sitter who checks in on him every day," I answered.

"So, not your boyfriend or partner?" he asked. *Woo-hoo!* I thought.

"I don't have one of those," I said, in an attempt to muster flirtatiousness.

"Me neither," he said, smiling.

Availability established, we still had a few challenges to sort out. First, Luis was working that night and couldn't leave to have dinner with me. Second, he didn't know when his shift would be over. It would depend on how busy the restaurant was. He made a reservation for me at an elegant restaurant nearby and we planned to meet later for after-dinner drinks. Plans made, we parted ways, dual-cheek kissing again for good measure.

Swooning, I drove to the incredibly fancy restaurant. It was a formal place, built into the sprawling rooms of an old mansion. Seated by the window, I had a beautiful view of the courtyard. Next to me was a table with two British couples, talking loudly. When I'm eating dinner by myself, it's hard not to accidentally overhear nearby conversations. I'm not trying to eavesdrop; sometimes, it just happens. In this specific situation, it was both unavoidable and unfortunate. It was unavoidable because of the volume of the conversation, and unfortunate given the topic: funerals and crematoriums. Not kidding. I cannot fathom why anyone would go out to eat at a beautiful restaurant while on vacation and talk about death, and in such specific detail. They had a lengthy conversation about the rules and processes of the crematorium. It was beyond bizarre. Clearly, this evening was to be a lesson in contrasts: my angry work persona vs. my happy adventuring persona. Life-affirming internal dialogue about meeting up with gorgeous sommelier vs. neighboring talks of death. Just par for the course, it seemed.

At one point, one of the women was returning to the table from the bathroom and made eye contact with me. I smiled at her and she stopped by my table before going back to her own.

"I'm not sure if you heard our earlier conversation? I'm so sorry to be so morbid over dinner!" she said.

Well, at least she recognized it was totally freaking crazy.

"Don't worry about it," I said, laughing. It seemed the polite response.

"Are you American?" she asked.

This led to the standard polite conversation that travelers have on the road. We talked about where we were all from, complimented each other's home countries, and commiserated over the state of the world. I learned that they were returning to this specific restaurant for the first time in over a decade and seemed quite lovely, despite the macabre nature of their previous discussion.

Meanwhile, Luis and I decided to meet at a local Irish pub about a ten minutes' drive from the restaurant. Arriving before him, I waited outside. As adventurous as I am, I am not exactly awesome at walking into bars by myself. Eating dinner alone doesn't bother me at all anymore, but bars flat-out intimidate me. When I eat by myself, at least I have a seat and a waiter assigned to take care of me. At a bar, I have to compete for space and attention, and this seems to poke at some underlying feeling of inadequacy or fear of rejection or similar. I always feel like I'm in some weird *Alice in Wonderland*-style world, where I am suddenly twenty feet tall and all the normal people in the bar can't help but gawk at me and my super-sized strangeness. It's terrible; my face gets all red and I just want to curl up in the fetal position under the nearest table.

While loitering outside this particular pub, a flash of red caught my attention. A striking young woman with russet brown hair and a bold red dress burst animatedly out of the pub gates.

"Do you have a light?" she asked me, with a halting British accent, a cigarette in her hand. Her voice was strangely melodious; it was as if a British angel was asking me to light her cigarette. Could this night get any stranger?

Staring at her incredulously, I managed to explain that I don't smoke and didn't have a light. She clearly found a light somewhere else because she returned to my side a few minutes later, smoking. A bizarre conversation ensued—gratefully, not about death. My new friend was an opera singer (who smokes?) from London. I mentioned how much I love

London and that I could totally live there again. She asked about the type of work I do and then, unbelievably, offered to connect me with her friend in London who runs marketing for Debenham's. We shared contact information and, just as quickly as she appeared, she disappeared back into the pub, never to be seen again. If we weren't now Facebook "friends," I would have thought she was an apparition.

Luis texted that he was running late, so I decided to brave the pub on my own. I braced myself for the awkwardness. Standing at the bar, I remembered the other reason I hate going to bars alone. Despite the fact that I feel like all eyes are on me, the reality is that I am short and have a quiet voice that doesn't project well. Ironically, as over-sized as I feel, I am practically invisible to bartenders, so it can take ages for one to realize I'm there and looking for a drink. The longer I wait, my already high-pitched voice turns squeakier, all but guaranteeing that my desperate beverage requests won't be heard. It's horrendous. Somehow, I caught this bartender's attention and ordered a Guinness, given that this was an Irish pub and all.

Totally exhausted from my beverage acquisition efforts, I headed to a tall table by the door so I would see Luis when he arrived. I was putting my wallet back in my purse when a lovely Irish brogue interrupted my deep breathing exercises.

"Is it worth it?" asked the very handsome thirty-something Irish man, pointing to my Guinness.

So, there's this theory among Guinness fans that the best Guinness can be found in Dublin, and that the quality declines the farther you get from there. From my perspective, Portugal is closer to Dublin than Connecticut is, so this should have been a better Guinness than I'm used to. For this guy, clearly from Ireland, it was dicey.

"Well, for me it is. I'm not so sure it will be for you," I replied.

I am actually still surprised by this relatively clever response, given my immense state of duress caused by procuring said Guinness. It was apparently a good answer because my new Irish friend laughed and decided to stick around to chat some more. He was quite charming, but I was distracted. Luis would be arriving at any moment and, here I was, at a table right by the door, ostensibly flirting with another European man while internally marveling that two European men had hit on me in one night and seriously thinking I needed to move to Europe. After a nice chat, he invited me to join him and his "boys" at the bar. I said I'd try to catch up with him later, and he went off with his boys.

What seemed like mere seconds later, Luis arrived. He was casually dressed now, in blue striped shorts and a white short-sleeved shirt that simultaneously highlighted both his deep olive tan and his biceps. How did he keep getting more gorgeous?

We walked back over to the bar so he could order a drink. Instantly, two loud German men jumped up excitedly and did that strange handshake/hug thing that guys do with Luis. They introduced themselves to me as well, but I was so confused by their enthusiasm that I didn't retain their names at all. It turns out that they were regular visitors to the Algarve and frequent guests at Luis's restaurant, and they were extremely curious to learn more about me since I was with Luis.

Clearly assuming we were a couple, one of the Germans asked how we had met. And this is how I got to hear the rather amazing "how we met" story from Luis's perspective.

"Well, I found Sara at a port wine lodge in Porto, in the north of Portugal," Luis said. *Swoon*. I mean, seriously, I was a puddle. He *found* me?

"I remember it so clearly," he continued. "She was visiting from America, and we both like the same types of wine. I kept coming back to talk to her. And then we discovered that she was going to be visiting the same hotel I would be working at here in Algarve and I knew we were meant to meet."

Oh my God. This gorgeous, wine-loving, *cat-loving* man thought we were meant to meet? Apparently, I had officially entered a parallel universe where this type of stuff actually happens to normal-looking, nerdy people like me.

Gratefully, the Germans were thrilled about this story and a welcome distraction from the swooning mess I was becoming. One of them gave me a bear hug, lifted me off the ground, and told me I clearly needed to move to Portugal now. Why wait to retire? He had a point.

Luis and I headed across the bar, looking for a table where we could finally sit and talk. On our way there, we were interrupted by a familiar, loud British man, one of the British Foursome who had been discussing crematoriums several hours ago at the fancy restaurant where I had eaten dinner. The complete Foursome, apparently having chosen the same place for an after-dinner drink, were assembled at a table near the bar, where the group's leader beckoned loudly to us.

"Where were you earlier?" he asked Luis, rather aggressively. Gesturing to me, he said, "She had to eat dinner all by herself!"

Luis was obviously rather confused by this verbal assault from a random, loud British man, so I explained that this man and his group had been sitting at the table next to me at dinner. And I explained to the British man that Luis was a sommelier and had to work during dinner.

"How did you two meet then?" asked the British man. I happily let Luis explain again how he found me in the north of Portugal.

Finally seated at a table free from interruptions, Luis and I settled in for a chat. We talked for a really long time about a really wide range of topics, including my tendency to quickly befriend other travelers that I meet at restaurants. He told me about the process to become a sommelier, and some of his prior jobs that led him to his current career path. Amazingly, we learned that we had crossed paths years before, when I stayed at a hotel where he worked in London. I told him about my job, and how I was increasingly unhappy with it and feeling unfulfilled—rather deep conversation for someone I hardly knew. It all felt so normal and comfortable. We might have come from very different places, but we had so much in common. As the conversation continued, we were leaning closer and closer to each other; partly due to the obvious attraction, but also in an effort to hear each other as the bar got increasingly rowdy. At one point, a very drunk Scottish man was standing on the table next to ours, singing at the top of his lungs. So, it didn't seem strange at all when Luis asked if I wanted to go somewhere quieter, where we could talk. Besides, I had my own rental car.

We left the pub and I followed Luis to his place, about twenty minutes' drive from the bar, but in the opposite direction from my hotel. His house had a courtyard in the back; Luis opened a ten-year-old bottle of local red wine and we sat outside, drinking and talking. It was fun to watch his excitement about the wine. I really enjoy watching experts at work, people who love what they do so much that you can feel it. Not only was I enjoying the wine, but I was double enjoying it as I also experienced it through Luis. We talked even more about our lives and the paths we had taken to get us where we were. Like me, Luis also believed that the Universe guides our direction and we need to listen to where it's leading; he "takes life as it comes." I said I needed a sign to tell me if I should move to Europe and we jokingly (and slightly drunkenly) concluded that missing my flight back to the US would be the sign that I was supposed to stay.

By now it was close to four in the morning, I'd had a Guinness and several glasses of wine and was an hour's drive away from my hotel. Clearly, it made more sense to just stay with Luis. And, well . . . I got back to my hotel at nearly ten, just as breakfast was ending. I felt like such a badass, being out all night, even though nothing really happened. In fact, literally sleeping with Luis instead of "sleeping with" Luis may turn out to be one of the biggest regrets of my life. I don't often meet insanely good-looking men who are actually nice and smart, too. I blame the Catholic Church. It's amazing what a Catholic upbringing can do to your openness to one-night stands, even with a gorgeous Portuguese sommelier. Sigh. I resolved to find a way to act differently the next time I end up in bed with a hot European sommelier.

The next day, it was time to drive to Lisbon for my flight to New York. I left extra early for the three-hour drive to make sure I had enough time to return my rental car. About an hour away from the airport, I decided to stop at a gas station to refill the car. When I got to the gas pump, I noticed a green handle indicating diesel, and then three handles to the right of the green handle. In the US, these would be the different grades of gasoline, so I assumed the same was true in Portugal. Spoiler alert: It's not.

I did notice that the leftmost handle had a sign above it that read, "*gasóleo.*" The one next to it read, "*gasolina.*" I didn't think much about it, and chose the leftmost one, which is what I would do in the US if I was refilling a rental car: Pick the cheapest gas. Yeah, so this was a super bad call. It turns out that "*gasóleo*" is actually also diesel, and my rental car ran on actual gasoline. Maybe three minutes out of the gas station, my car started to sputter and the engine light started to flash furiously. I pulled the car over into the shoulder just as it sputtered to a stop. Initially, I didn't understand what had happened until I noticed the little sticker next to the car's gas valve that said, "*gasolina*." I was now an hour away from the airport in a car that I had misfueled.

I quickly dug out my car rental paperwork and started calling every number I could find, finally finding someone who spoke English. I wanted to call a taxi to take me to the airport right away but learned I had to wait for the tow truck before I could leave; otherwise, I would be liable for any damage that happened to the car while it sat, alone and untended, on the side of the highway. Oh, and it would take at least an hour for the tow truck to arrive. I was literally stuck.

This was absolutely one of the worst experiences in my life. Standing on the side of the highway in a country where I didn't speak the language, as cars raced by me, having no idea if or when I'd be rescued, just watching the time tick down to my flight departure. I had no idea if I had ruined the car and what I'd be charged for that; no idea if I'd make my flight; no idea what I'd do if I didn't. After more than an hour of waiting in suspended and intense anxiety, the tow truck and taxi finally arrived. I convinced the taxi driver to drive as fast as he could, but it was too late; when I got to the airport, boarding had closed. I called my airline and there were no other flights to New York until the next day. Knowing that my boss would eviscerate me if I took another day off, I searched and found another airline that had space available and paid out of pocket for a one-way ticket to New

York, leaving about five hours later than I should have. All things considered, it could have been much worse.

Still shaken from the morning's drama, and now with plenty of time on my hands, I decided to soothe my anxiety with caffeine and food. I bought a double shot of espresso, a giant Iberian ham sandwich, and a famous Portuguese egg custard tart called *pastel de nata* and sat down in the central courtyard of the airport to attempt to process the insanity of the day. Despite my terrible morning, I was kind of amazed that I had successfully resolved such an absurd problem on my own. I thought back to the mortifying way I had handled myself when I met Michael Bublé and the uber paranoia of my early solo traveling days. Solving this crazy and totally unexpected problem with just a few hours' delayed return seemed almost remarkable. In general, I don't think I see my own growth while I'm growing, but it suddenly seemed impossible to un-see.

And then something else occurred to me: Less than forty-eight hours earlier, I had been drinking wine with a gorgeous Portuguese sommelier who likes cats and believes that the Universe gives you signs, discussing how *missing my flight* would be the sign that I should stay in Europe. And I had never missed a flight in my entire frequent-flying life. Until now.

Call me crazy, but I think that's a sign.

Iceland: The (Christmas) Cat's Meow

I started traveling to Iceland before anyone who wasn't Icelandic traveled there on purpose. More than an incredible destination, Iceland represents my evolution as a traveler and, also, as a person.

I first visited Iceland with a college friend, less than a year after graduation, when my relationship with my then-future husband had just started getting serious. My second trip to Iceland, a few years after my divorce, was all about flexing my travel muscles in a somewhat ridiculous display of my newly reclaimed independence. And my third and most recent trip was the one where I finally got my brain around taking my next big leap.

While it seems completely fantastical in the context of the current Icelandic tourism boom, Icelandair was practically bribing travelers to stay in Reykjavík with comically low fares when I booked my first trip. Those were also the days shortly after I graduated from college, when every penny I earned funded school loans or the outrageous rent I paid for what can best be described as a makeshift treehouse illegally constructed within a very legal and very expensive Upper West Side Manhattan apartment. The treehouse, complete with a ceiling as short as I am and window blinds duct-taped to the ceiling for "privacy," enabled the sharing of the 250-square-foot space with another human, who could squeeze in below. I was completely and totally broke.

My friend, Liane, suggested we go on a spring break trip, but there was no way I could afford it. She did some research and came back with a solution—Iceland! The whole week-long trip, including flight and hotel and several group tours, would be under five hundred dollars per person with the latest, palm greasing Icelandair offer. I didn't have five hundred dollars, but I had a job, a credit card, a deep love for a great deal and a burning desire to go somewhere, so I said yes without really thinking about it.

As soon as the flight approached the runway at the Reykjavík airport, it became clear that we were in for an adventure. First, it was a complete blizzard; we could barely see the ground as the landing gear lowered. While this was disconcerting, it was quickly followed by abject panic when I began to distinguish the ground. On either side of the narrow runway, all I could see was jagged black rock, definitely not a place that seemed safe to land a plane.

"What is all this black rock?" Liane wondered aloud.

Suddenly, a disturbing potential answer occurred to me.

"I think it might be lava?" I sort of answered and asked at the same time.

"Wait, we're landing in a lava field?" Liane's voice had jumped a few octaves.

Once we were off of the plane, now standing in said lava field, I realized I had never been colder in my entire life.

Apparently, four years in the wilds of New Hampshire do not compare to your average March in Iceland.

Highlights of our trip included tours to several astoundingly vast waterfalls, including the famous Gullfoss and Skógafoss, a visit to see Geysir, after which all geysers are named, the black sand beaches of Vik and the infamous Blue Lagoon geothermal spa. I remember standing in snow up to my thighs, marveling at waterfalls that seemed to originate in the sky. Gullfoss was particularly amazing. A multi-level waterfall shaped like an enormous, curved staircase, it seemed more like a cinematic special effect than an actual geological structure.

At the nearby geothermal park, we learned that Geysir no longer erupts and waited instead to see the nearby geyser, Strokkur, put on a show. I was holding my camera tightly when I felt the earth start to rumble—it was kind of like the sound an air conditioner makes when it starts up coupled with a deep vibration under your feet. The sound and vibration comingled and grew bigger and bolder, culminating in a thunderous roar and an explosion of water, kind of like a sulfury firehose shooting up from the center of the earth. Needless to say, I dropped my camera. Luckily, Strokkur erupts every ten minutes or so and, on the third try, I got my picture (which is still hanging in my apartment). I thought it was totally worth the wait, but Liane may disagree.

For me, the most memorable experience on that trip was our visit to the Blue Lagoon, a man-made geothermal spa with an outdoor pool built into the lava. It was the coolest thing because I entered the outdoor pool from the inside. A very small part of the pool was indoors and the external wall of the building actually went through the pool. I walked through a door in this wall to get outside. It was also amazing because it was snowing outside. Surrounded by lava while standing in an outdoor geothermal pool that was about eighty degrees when the air temperature was about zero degrees during a snowstorm, absolutely nothing made sense and it was awesome. In the cloud of steam hovering over the pool, visibility was limited to what was immediately in front of me. It was like being in a strangely multi-temperate cocoon.

Because this was before tourists discovered Iceland, the Blue Lagoon was pretty empty. Suddenly, I heard American English, the first time I had heard an American in Iceland who was not Liane. We couldn't see the Americans in the steam, but we followed their voices and eventually found them—a retired couple on their way to the UK who couldn't resist Icelandair's amazing deals. Not long after, another American duo emerged from the steam into our midst (and mist) and we had a small quorum of cheap, adventurous Americans in a geothermal spa in the middle of a snowstorm. Just another day in Iceland.

Fast forward about fifteen years. It was June and I had just finished a yoga class in Connecticut. A lot had changed in my life since Iceland Trip Number One: I'd gotten married and divorced, gone to graduate school, changed careers, moved ten times—and was now in the beginning phases of a mid-life crisis. Suddenly deeply aware of my own mortality and vastly more at ease with flying solo, it required very little encouragement to prompt an adventure.

As class was ending, the instructor, who is also a golfer, invited us to attend an upcoming summer solstice class celebrating the longest day of the year unless we'd "be golfing at midnight in Iceland." She clarified that Iceland had a midnight golf tournament on summer solstice because it is so far north that the sun doesn't really set. Suddenly, inspiration struck. I don't golf, but I really wanted to experience the sun not setting!

I thought about this for about fifteen minutes, which was how long it took me to drive home. As soon as I got into my apartment, I booked the flights. Life is short, right? My ridiculous itinerary included twenty-six hours in Iceland, just enough time to see the midnight sun not-set and no vacation days needed.

Planning such a trip a few days before going leads to very fun water cooler conversations in the office:

"Any plans for the weekend?"

"Yes, I'm going to Iceland."

"Nice, for how long?"

"Oh, for the weekend. I'm going to see the midnight sun!"

"You're going to Iceland for a weekend?"

"Why not? It's the summer solstice!"

Turns out that not so many people outside of yoga circles pay much attention to the solstices.

Arriving early that Saturday morning, I was happy to see the familiar lava field and even happier that it was not snowing. I went to the hotel, dropped off my bags and set out to re-acquaint myself with Reykjavík. I wandered down the main shopping street and straight into a parade complete with marching bands and Icelandic horses. Apparently, it was Iceland Independence Day. Also, Icelandic horses are absolutely adorable, pony-sized, and extra furry to withstand the Icelandic winters.

Around 6:00 p.m., I arrived at the meeting point for my Midnight Sun tour. The plan was to visit the Secret Lagoon, a smaller and more natural geothermal pool than the Blue Lagoon, dine at a local restaurant and visit the famous Gullfoss waterfall around midnight since the sun wouldn't be setting. Only one other person was waiting—an extremely inquisitive American college student on a layover before catching a flight to Munich. In fact, she was the most inquisitive person I had ever met, asking questions about everything and giggling after each one. After about five minutes of talking to (answering?) her, I was very excited for other people to join our tour. Unfortunately, I was out of luck; it was just the two of us and our tour guide, really taking the idea of the longest day of the year to new levels. On the plus side, her constant questions revealed some interesting insight into Icelandic culture that probably wouldn't have made the guidebooks. Specifically, I learned that Iceland's population and gene pool are so small that Icelanders have an app on their phones to make sure they're not related to each other when they meet in bars and want to hook up. An accidental incest-prevention app? Who knew?

After a relaxing float in the geothermal pool and a festive dinner (I invited the tour guide and the owners of the restaurant to join us to stave off the incessant questioning), we journeyed to the Gullfoss waterfall. Arriving there was totally disorienting. The last time I had seen this vast waterfall, everything was covered in snow and I feared losing limbs to frostbite. Now, it was nearly midnight and it was warm and *sunny.* I was so excited, I raced out of the van and up to the highest lookout point to take in the whole scene. Unbeknownst to me, my chatty tour partner had followed. Somehow, this turned into a frenetic photo shoot where we took pictures of each other in increasingly bizarre poses alongside the falls under the midnight sun. I may not have joined in on the questioning, but I definitely embraced the giggling. I still feel bad for that tour guide.

A few years later, Iceland crossed my travel path again. I am on a lifelong quest to win at New Year's Eve (see "Switzerland via Snowplow") and decided to again try traveling somewhere exciting to celebrate. I googled, "best places to celebrate New Year's Eve" and, much to my surprise, Reykjavík, Iceland, popped up. Apparently, Reykjavík was home to an "organic" fireworks display where locals gathered in the main square to shoot fireworks at midnight. This seemed slightly dangerous, but the pictures looked beautiful and Iceland is only about a five-hour flight from New York, so why not? This led to Iceland Trip Number Three.

Arriving in Reykjavík for the third time, I was nonplussed by the lava field landing area. It was surprising not to see snow in Iceland in December (global warming, anyone?), but I was ready for anything and looking forward to this latest go at a non-crap New Year's Eve. I checked into my hotel, dropped off my bags, and hit the incredibly dark streets. It was about 10:00 a.m. and it was basically night. In late December, there were just a few hours of daylight. As I wandered, I admired the holiday decorations in all the shop windows—Christmas trees and lights and elves and . . . black cats? At first, I didn't think much of it. I mean, I love cats. If I owned a shop, I'd probably try to include cats in the décor in some way. I made a mental note to do so in my own holiday decorations. But the cats were literally everywhere, in every window, in every shop and residence on the street. One shop had a particularly enormous black cat decal in the window and what appeared to be a collection of cat merchandise, so I went in. The incredibly stunning Viking store clerk saw me admiring all the cat stuff.

"Do you like the Christmas Cat?" he asked.

I admitted that I was unfamiliar with this particular legend, but quite curious to learn more.

"Ah, I've lived my whole life in Iceland. I forget it is not typical to see cats for Christmas," he said. "Would you like me to tell you about the legend?"

I was definitely interested in storytelling with this particular Viking. Didn't the Nordic people create oral history traditions? Honestly, I don't know and it doesn't matter. What I do know is that I will never say no when a very hot man wants to talk to me about cats.

This is what I learned. In Iceland, there isn't one Santa. Instead, twelve mischievous Christmas elves play pranks leading up to Christmas. Their mom is a witch and their pet is, of course, the Christmas Cat. For reasons neither my new Viking friend nor I understood, the Christmas Cat comes down from the mountains every Christmas to eat children who do not get new clothes as Christmas gifts. (Was this legend created by textile merchants?) I also learned that there was a giant, lighted sculpture of the Christmas Cat in the main square that I clearly needed to check out.

Leaving the store with some (a lot of) Christmas Cat merchandise, I headed toward the sculpture. It did not disappoint. Enormous, with evil red eyes and in full attack mode with a deeply arched back and unsheathed claws, it appeared to be ready to pounce on anyone who crossed the street. It reminded me of a demonic version of my sweet kitty, Lou, who lacks red eyes and any intent to kill anything other than laser lights. Lou is also not fond of children, but instead of trying to eat them, he cowers under the coffee table in their presence. I found myself simultaneously delighted and bemused by this new connection with Iceland. Really, a Christmas Cat? How had I never heard about this in all my crazy-cat-lady years? I deemed myself an honorary Icelander and decided to reward myself with something sweet to eat.

Walking into a bakery just off the main square, I was shocked to discover a yummy-looking cookie labeled, in English, the "Sara," which is my name. So, I ordered myself and took a seat in the café to collect my thoughts. It turns out that I am delicious, chocolate filled, and frosted. I contemplated a country that celebrates Christmas with cats and cookies bearing my name. Another moment where the Universe seemed to be telling me I was in the right place. Or, perhaps, that I was Icelandic in a past life.

After a freezing day in Iceland, I decided to warm up with a return trip to the Blue Lagoon. It had most definitely changed since my first visit. First, it was a madhouse with tourists. Second, the lagoon itself was like fifty times bigger and included two in-lagoon bars—one serving drinks and another selling a menu of expensive face masks made from local mud.

I was still able to enter the lagoon via the indoor/outdoor water door. Once outside, it looked like I was standing at the edge of a lake and I decided to explore the now huge expanse. Moving slowly through the water that felt heavy with the weight of its minerals, I discovered saunas and heated waterfalls. I passed the mask bar, where attendants wearing white lab coats stood inside a heated nook, scooping portions of various masks into the hands of customers, who then applied the mud to their faces. I spotted the main bar and walk-floated toward it. It seemed a bit too early to start drinking, even on vacation, so I decided to try a smoothie made with carrots and ginger. I wandered the full expanse with my smoothie in hand, my body in an underwater cocoon while my face and beverage-holding hand dealt with the cold and sounds of a packed community pool. It was like my head and heart were in different realities.

In the spirit of unification, I concluded that it wasn't actually too early to drink and headed back to the bar, where I ordered prosecco. I found a quiet, shallow corner of the lagoon, in the shadows of the bar, where I could sit in the water and take in the world around me. It was one of those most precious travel moments, the ones that are so quintessential you can close your eyes and pull them into your memory on command and feel like you are back in that exact moment. When I close my eyes, I can still feel the warmth of the water, the effervescence of the prosecco, the cold of the air and the energy of the environment. I can hear the cacophony of voices surrounding me. It was peaceful and soothing and calm, the perfect way to end a crazy year.

Finishing my prosecco, I began the slow wander back to the door when a voice I recognized jolted me out of my chill reverie. Not three feet away from me, practically in the middle of the Blue Lagoon, was one of my favorite New York City-based celebrity chefs. I watched her on Food Network, had been to her restaurants, and was completely stunned to see her in person in Iceland; I stopped in my tracks and said an awkward hello. As much as things had changed, running into unexpected travelers in the Blue Lagoon apparently hadn't. Just a typical day in Iceland.

And then it was New Year's Eve, my holiday nemesis. I travel by myself so often now that I don't really consider solo travel to be a big deal anymore, but even I had to acknowledge that spending New Year's Eve alone in a foreign country was a bit on the bold side. And to me, bold actions require bolder outfits, so I found the boldest possible option—a black sequined jumpsuit. With head-to-toe sequins on a one-piece, long-sleeved jumpsuit with fitted cuffs at the wrists and ankles and a dramatic adjustable zipper neckline, it was kind of like NASA met Studio 54. It was spectacular. I paired it with similarly bold red lipstick and had the strange realization that I really felt like myself, which seemed vaguely problematic that it took sequins and a bold lip to accomplish this. Dressed to kill (or blind), I departed for the evening's events: a classical music concert at the iconic Hallgrímskirkja church, dinner at a traditional Icelandic restaurant, and fireworks back at the church square.

While I don't really like classical music—it makes me angry, though I've never been sure why—I do really like unique architecture and was happy to have a good reason to hang out in the quirky church. From the outside entrance, behind an imposing statue of Leif Erikson, America's favorite Viking, the church spire looks like two steep staircases that start impractically high were smashed together at the top. For some reason, it reminds me of the pigtails of the girl in the Wendy's logo, minus the orange. The concert, featuring two local trumpeters and the church organist playing festive holiday music, was unexpectedly, an absolute delight. The church was filled with well-dressed local families celebrating together, and their upbeat energy matched the music. I think I smiled for the entire concert; my face hurt when it ended. So far, so good!

From there, I headed to dinner, now cautiously optimistic about the evening despite it being New Year's Eve. After a delicious meal, I was relaxing into a decadent food coma and swirling my dessert wine in my glass when my thoughts were interrupted by one half of the gay Canadian couple who had been enjoying dinner at a nearby table. I had decided earlier that evening that they must be Canadian because, like most of the rest of the world, I believe polite and friendly non-British-English speakers must be Canadians and not Americans.

"I hope you don't mind, but I had to stop by before we left. I had to tell you that you are just the picture of elegance! The picture!"

Surprised, I thanked him profusely and told him he had made my night while silently wondering if sequins really are elegant and if excessive wine drinking could cause hallucinations. Clearly, I had entered some sort of bizarr-o world where I liked classical music and black-sequined jumpsuits were elegant. And where New Year's Eve was not yet sucking.

Now it was time for the fireworks. The fireworks in Reykjavík are not an organized display like Americans are used to seeing for holidays or at minor league baseball stadiums desperate to drive up attendance. Apparently, fireworks are generally illegal in Iceland, except for the weeks leading up to New Year's Eve, when they are sold to raise money for charities. Around midnight, everyone goes to the church square in Reykjavík, shoots off their own fireworks and somehow, no one gets killed. Unsure of what to expect, I walked to the square a little after 11:00 p.m. It was pleasantly crowded with enough people to make it feel like an event but not enough to feel claustrophobic.

I heard every language and accent around me—British and Irish accents combined with German and Italian and Spanish and Portuguese and Chinese and everything in between. Around 11:30 p.m. the first fireworks started with increasing intensity as midnight approached. There was no structure to what was happening; it just seemed like a bunch of people from across the globe found a way to safely coordinate with explosives. Suddenly, the whole crowd started counting down and then the church bells tolled, and the fireworks exploded in complete madness from all directions—a near-constant flurry of stunning bursts of light in front of the church, to the sides, from behind, even from distant parts of the city. It was organic and beautiful and insane! And it continued at this pace until nearly 12:30 a.m., when the crowd started to dissipate. The experience was amazing, the energy was tremendous, and I was the happiest I'd ever been on New Year's Eve by far.

Not wanting the night to end, I decided to experience more of Reykjavík's famous nightlife. I found an Irish pub nearby and stopped in for a nightcap in the form of a pint of Guinness. I tucked myself into a relatively quiet corner of the crowded bar while the Irish band surprised me by playing a bunch of American "classics," including two Backstreet Boys songs and a few by John Denver. There was something reassuring about hearing an Irish singer in Iceland sing the American songs I grew up with while a bar full of people from everywhere sang along. The world really is much smaller than it seems, and we really do have more in common than we think. And there really is power in words, sung or spoken, to bring us all together.

After dodging a bunch of seriously drunk people staggering home on the short walk back to my hotel—I saw one guy weave across the sidewalk and walk right into a lamppost—it seemed another nightcap was in order in the hotel's lobby bar. As I drank my first prosecco of the new year and reflected on this once-in-a-lifetime evening, Post Malone's song "Circles" started playing. Although the song is about escaping a bad relationship, and I avoid this problem by avoiding dating relationships altogether, the idea of letting go struck a chord (pun intended).

For years, I'd been contemplating that I lived two different lives: my "real" life, at "home" in the US, where I worked too much and was generally miserable, and my travel life, where I was on the road and happy and my best and favorite self (and, occasionally, "the picture of elegance"). In my heart, I wanted to move to Europe, but the idea of letting go of my miserable real life always terrified me. How would I pay my bills? What about health care? Could I live so far away from my family? Also, possibly even more worrisome, what would happen if I lived in or near the places where I loved to travel? Which me would I be? Would work me resurface on a new continent, or would travel me need to figure out how to work? Was it possible to merge and be just one more authentic me, the best of both?

Looking out on the Reykjavík streets, alive with the energy of the people and the lights and the possibility, I found myself thinking I was ready to let go of the fear and this identity that had become so stifling. It suddenly seemed like the right time for my next grand adventure. I was wearing the perfect outfit to get started.

The Other Half of Single

―――――

"*Why are you still single?*"

For many years, this question had been my nemesis. It was really the inclusion of the word, "still," that made it seem less like a question and more like an accusation. "Still" single felt like a judgment of my single status, evaluating single to be both inferior to being partnered and a status that, once entered, should be exited as quickly as possible. The question seemed impossible to answer appropriately, and I spent years fumbling for a response that wouldn't leave me or the often unknowingly insensitive questioner feeling bad about my life, with varying degrees of success:

My response	How I felt after responding in this manner	Impact to (insensitive) questioner
Sobbing (yes, this happened. Someone actually posed this question early in my divorce; not cool.)	The definition of pathetic	Massive pity
I really don't know. Do you have any ideas?	Pathetic with a dash of desperate	Serious pity
Well, I guess I just haven't met the right one yet...	Pathetic and trite	Pity
Do you have any friends to set me up with?	Equal (large) portions, pathetic and desperate	Pity mixed with misplaced sense of obligation
All men are assholes	Angry	Internal ringing of "bitter divorced woman" alarm bells

Until, one fateful day, when something amazing happened.

Questioner: "Why are you still single?"

Me: "Because I choose to be!"

What?

I'm not sure who was more surprised by that response, but it felt incredible. Gone was the sinking feeling of lameness, replaced with a clear sense of empowerment! And the look on the question-asker's face was priceless. He was clearly caught off guard; no pity was coming at me this time. He was actually curious and, possibly, a tad envious? I felt my posture straighten and a newfound desire to cross my wrists Wonder Woman-style and send out blasts of happy laser beam sunshine on behalf of singletons everywhere. At the very least, my unexpected response certainly prompted some self-reflection.

Strictly speaking, I didn't exactly choose to be single, at least not initially. And initially, I felt terrible about it. I had bought into the myths that American society teaches us about marriage, i.e., that marriage is necessary for a happy and secure future free of loneliness. When I got married at twenty-five, I most certainly thought I was securing my future happiness and that I wouldn't grow old alone. And I made a lot of personal and professional choices to support my married lifestyle that I never would have made had I been single; moving multiples times to cities I wouldn't have chosen, taking jobs I didn't want or like to be able to live with my husband.

Probably the worst of these moves happened when my husband got his first job after graduate school. For me, where I live is critically important. I like diverse, urban communities, with lots of restaurants and cultural activities that I can walk to. Whenever I watch *House Hunters*, I am always rooting for the slightly smaller, slightly more expensive, city center apartment. To me, this is the ideal way to live, to be in the heart of things.

My husband's job was in a rural, conservative community in central Virginia. It was neither diverse nor urban, and all the restaurants were chains. The only cultural activities were churches. I needed a car to go anywhere. I also had to give up my job in a preeminent bank to make this move. I'll never forget how dejected I felt when we arrived to look for apartments. It was a nightmare, filled with cookie-cutter "apartment communities."

We finally selected an apartment and met with the leasing agent to sign the new lease. My husband and I each signed and printed our names. The leasing agent wrinkled her nose in confusion.

"I thought y'all were married?" she asked us. There was a sense of suspicion in the air.

"We are," answered my husband, looking confused.

"But y'all have different names!" she exclaimed.

"I didn't change my name when we got married," I said.

"Oh, honey," the leasing agent said. "You better get on that, girl. You don't want people around here thinking you aren't married."

I felt the sinking sensation of dread that had been with me all day twist into a knot of misery. It was bad enough that I had to live in this God-forsaken "apartment community." Would I lose my entire identity, too? I must have looked angry because my husband grabbed my hand and rushed us out of the office, likely before I could embarrass him further.

I hated every second I spent in that apartment and committed myself to my graduate school applications to get the hell out. That was always the plan: I would support my husband through grad school and then he would support me when it was my turn. So, I applied and was accepted and—surprise—my husband wouldn't make the move. He had a new job, after all, and he needed to stay. But I could move four hours away to Philadelphia alone if I wanted to go, and he would support me from afar.

It was a difficult decision, but I ultimately chose to go back to school. We were still married but living apart, and for me, it was constant stress. I felt conflicted about pursuing my dreams away from my husband and angry that he couldn't support me in the way I had supported him. I probably should have realized then that the marriage wasn't working, but I couldn't let go of this cultural narrative about marriage. 'Til death do us part, right? Instead, I spent the two years of grad school feeling guilty and traveling to see my husband almost every weekend while he visited me twice.

I sacrificed a lot, and quite honestly, the best parts of myself, to be married. The parts of myself that I like the most—my enthusiastic curiosity and adventurousness, the joy I feel when I learn or experience something new—didn't fit the traditional model or my ex's expectations for building a stable, secure life. While my natural inclination was to travel and discover and grow, his was to stay and build and conform. And despite all this sacrifice, shortly after I finished graduate school, I found myself alone, in another city I wouldn't have chosen, having to make the best of it with inconsiderate people asking me why I was still single.

I'll never forget how awful that initial alone period was. How afraid I was when I stopped wearing my wedding rings. That sense of protection from unwanted advances, of being validated by someone's choice of me as partner, of security, was suddenly gone.

Slowly, I began to put my pieces back together again, to rediscover who I was and what really mattered to me. I rediscovered my sense of adventure, my need to explore and learn, my ability to connect. And, while mourning the security I had lost, I eventually came to realize that it was never real in the first place. There's no such thing. No one person can prevent you from feeling lonely. No one person can protect you.

I also realized the joy and empowerment that came from making my own decisions. Sure, no one is here to rescue me, but no one is here to control me, either. I'd rather be empowered to choose even though that means I am also empowered to choose badly. At least they are my choices. Much to my surprise, I realized I was actually happier being single than I had been when I was married. For the first time in my adult life, I could live authentically without that nagging need to accommodate. And the adventure is both more real and more exciting than the "security" ever was.

I guess, technically, even now, I'm not exactly choosing to be single. I am choosing to embrace where I am in life right now and that I don't know exactly where the journey will take me, or with whom. Or, as one of my friends likes to say, I am choosing to do shit on my own terms to be happy. I'm not closing the door on dating or relationships, or even marriage. I really am quite the closet romantic. In fact, I may be wearing a t-shirt that says "Happy Hour is any hour I'm watching the Hallmark Channel" as I write this.

My hyperactive imagination, both a blessing and a curse, has created fascinating daydreams featuring me and a handsome European man (he's Italian, Greek, or Portuguese; I haven't decided) holding hands and running through a vineyard in the rain. I'm not sure why it's raining; I think it has something to do with *The Notebook*. And a very clear image of a wedding on a specific balcony in Santorini at sunset, wearing an off-white sheath dress with a plunging neckline, where I would state my vows in the language of my beloved, which I currently don't speak since I don't know which language to learn to speak to an unknown future fiancé. I also envision him cooking me home-made gnocchi in a beautiful villa by the sea, which I guess means he must be Italian because it's always gnocchi; I love gnocchi.

Anyway, the point is that I'm not averse to the idea of partnership; if I meet the right person, a true partner I want to share the journey with, I could be convinced. But I know the sacrifices needed to make a relationship work, and for right now, that's not for me. I am happy to be as I am and excited for whatever my future holds, alone or partnered. I embrace the possibility that comes with uncertainty.

Not long ago, I was organizing an impromptu happy hour at work and stopped by a colleague's office to see if he wanted to join. He said he needed to check in with his "other half" first. This got me thinking: What is the other half of single? I like to think of myself as complete as I am, not needing another person to make me whole. My single life has enabled countless adventures and they are the gifts that keep on giving, the memories that make me smile on my darkest days, the friendships around the world that I cherish.

I've had so many incredible experiences that they didn't all make it in this book, including flying in a helicopter above an erupting volcano in Hawaii on my fortieth birthday while successfully not vomiting on the pilot, riding in the back of a pickup truck with a film crew and pulling a minivan along the streets of Auckland while filming a commercial where New Zealanders pretend to be Americans singing about their love of hummus, and seeing my life flash before my eyes (complete with the accompanying awesomely weird obituary) while successfully managing to not drive a dogsled off a cliff in northern Finland. I've formed deep connections on nearly every corner of the globe—multiple adopted families, a German friend who has always seemed uncannily like a long-lost sister, an advertising executive-turned-yoga-instructor in Santorini who has become my de facto spiritual advisor. I'm certain these experiences and relationships would not have been possible had I been traditionally partnered.

So, what is the other half of single? For me, it's freedom, independence, and endless choices. It's knowing I get stronger and more capable every day the more I live and do on my own. It's travel and cats and yoga and eating cheese plates for dinner on multiple continents. It's a pantry full of shoes instead of food because why not? It's creating my own definition of family, where family can be actual family or friends or people from the other side of the world who instantly just get me. It's about crossing paths and connecting and experiencing the journey, wherever it leads. It's the beautiful adventures that make me cherish my life and this amazing world, and make me feel blessed and complete and whole. It's the life I love.

Epilogue

On New Year's Eve 2019 in Iceland, when I was blissfully unaware that the world was about to fall apart, I decided I was finally ready to take a big leap and fulfill a life-long dream of moving to Europe. Earlier that year, I learned that it was possible for me to apply for Italian citizenship thanks to my great-grandparents. Because they were Italian citizens and Italian citizenship is based on bloodlines and not birth location, I could reclaim my Italian citizenship through them even though I was born in the US. Confusing, but, as I would later come to appreciate, most Italian legal things are.

The experiences described in this book, as well as my post-divorce travels to twenty more countries that didn't make these pages, gave me the confidence to think I could actually pull off this move alone before even learning to speak Italian. My first solo trip to Amsterdam helped me understand that I could not only navigate safely while solo but also experience joy. Falling in love with Santorini taught me that powerful connections can exist beyond those between people. My time in Naples just scratched the surface of my connection with my cultural heritage, and I knew I needed to delve deeper into all things Italian. Missing my flight in

Portugal was the wake-up call I needed to seriously consider making my dream a reality. Seeing my own evolution through my three trips to Iceland made it clear to me that I needed a big change, a life change, to align my real life with my travel life and be my truest self.

Friends often ask me if I've forgiven my ex-husband. Strangely, with all that has happened, I find myself feeling thankful toward him. I am so much happier now than I could ever have imagined being before. And I was so entrenched in the social norms that told me being married was the preferred state of things that I don't think I would have had the courage to end our marriage, even though I'm not sure I was ever really happy being married. So, while I wish things had ended more kindly, I am really happy they ended. Being single has made it possible for me to be me. And as a single person, I have the ultimate freedom to go where life calls.

The pandemic delayed me slightly, but my cat, Lou, and I made the move to Tuscany. It's been an amazing adventure—for both of us, actually. Every morning, I look out my windows onto my medieval street with this feeling I can only describe as pure delight. Part of me still can't believe I really did it. But all of me is sure I have a lot more stories to tell.

Acknowledgments

M y book journey confirms that "single" and "alone" are not synonyms! So many people have helped make this dream a reality, and I am forever grateful. A special thank you to Cheryl Cuglewski, Suzanne Lenzer, Coreen McGann, Lisa and Rich Phillips, and Kerry Powers, for their early insights, perspective, advice, feedback, and encouragement—not to mention, the sanity checks. Thank you also to Amy Foust, for the quote that started it all (and for not calling the police).

None of this would have been possible without the support of the teams at the Creator Institute and New Degree Press, especially Eric Koester and Nicole Spindler; and my brilliant editors, Katie Sigler and Kathy Wood. Kathy, epilogues will always make me blush thanks to you. Thank you also to Linda Berardelli for believing in my vision.

My heartfelt thanks to the following people who believed in me even before they could read this book: Fed Arreola, Laura Artz, Sharon Ayer, Dan Baker, Penelope Barnett, Liane Bennett, Betsy Benning, Nelly Bentz, Cris Benvenuto, Sarah Bergers, Allison Bergstrom, Marisa Blubaugh, Sylvia Borowski, Alyssa Braca, Christopher Braca, Daniel Braca, Stacey Brenner, Christine Bystrov, Christina Caprice, Michelle

Carmell, Erin Catalina, Neil Chawhan, Stacey Chiappetta, Yossi Ciment, Margaret Clayton, Annabella Colletti, Monica Colman, Amanda Cox, John Crerand, Jim (Dad 2) and Pat Cuglewski, Luiz DePaula, Keily DiBugnara, Paula Doroff, Allison English, Ray Fields, Krysten Fingers, Colleen Flaherty, Lisa Flemming, Janet Flenniken, Stephen Ford, Brad Frankel, Joe Franzino, Beth Freeman, Sara Gable, Michelle Gans, Kristin Garro, Leslie Garrone, Amanda Gelly, Noel Geoffroy, Jessica George, Joe Giallanella, Lily Goldshore, Evelyn Graeff, Caroline Graham, Rachel Graper, Sharyn Green, Roger Griesmeyer, Catie Grimes, Jen Haberman, Nicci Hafer, Michele Hall, Megan Hennigan, Sara Hewitt, Susan Hickey, Cheryl Hoefs, Addison Holcomb, Andrea Holtzman, Laura Hoye, Andrea Hulse, Katie Ingram, Raj Jain, Ruo Jing, Jennifer Jones, Gemma Jorda, Lisa Kahn, Alaina Kane, Amit Kapoor, Deb Karcher, Dennis Katsnelson, Andrea Kavouklis, JoAnn Kazimer, Dawn Kerr, Ricky Khetarpaul, Rosse Kiss, Eric Koester, Anat Kornberg, Bessie Kotsifas, Katie Lachter, Kimberly Lang, Brian Lauzon, Beryl Lawrence, Dominique Lazanski, Gouri LeDonne, Jason Levine, Joyce Liao, Helen Lukash, Caitlin Mahler, Chris Mancinelli, Marisa Mariani, Melissa Mason, Rosie McGovern, Alexis Medina, Nancy Medina, Laura Messerschmidt, Tina Michaels, Erica Michelstein, Cheryl Mikolay, Lucia Monacelli, Caitlin Monoscalco, Rick Monteith, Jennifer Mrzlack, Dave Muhlenfeld, CarmenMaria Navarro, Elizabeth Nordlie, Mel Novak, Lara O'Brien, Galina Orlosky, Lindsey Paola, Neha Parikh, Samantha Parker, Garima Pathak, Melissa Perez, Eugenio Perrier, Tony Perry, Holly Peterman, Steve Platt, Katie Polk, Louise Prader, Rebecca Prestel, Julie Price, Larry Quartana, Luisa Ramondo, Lisa Rousseau, Kristen Royal, Stephanie Rubeo, Timothea Ryan, Elizabeth Salter, Emily Sands, Gabi

Sarhos, Kelly Savino, Amy Schoemaker, Brendan Schuetze, Christine Seaman-Shakoor, Katie Segall, Shali Shalit-Shoval, Lifan Shen, Anat Shiwak-Harry, Michael Shoretz, Rick Shuman, Terri Sobel, Cynthia Sosa, Kimberly Stahl, Jen Stark, Chandler Stroud, Sarah Sugarman, Michelle Sweetser, Kelsey Tanaka, Dominique Toublan, Sigalit Vacnich, Richard Viens, Jacqueline Villamil, Anke von Geldern, Robin Wardle, Emily Watson, Patricia Werhahn, Barbara Whipple, Brian Wortham, Suzanne Wuebben, Jennifer Yanavage, Andri Yennari, Robert Young, Jill Yung, and Lex Zaharoff.

Last but not least, thanks to Chapstick, Twinkie, and Lou.

Appendix

Author's Note

Keegan, Marina. *The Opposite of Loneliness: Essays and Stories*. New York: Scribner, 2014.

US Census Bureau. "America's Families and Living Arrangements: 2020." Table H1. Households by Type and Tenure of Householder for Selected Characteristics: 2020. Accessed January 4, 2022.
https://www.census.gov/data/tables/2020/demo/families/cps-2020.html.

Altars Ablaze!

Best Place to Live. s.v. "Shelton, Connecticut." Accessed June 10, 2022.
https://www.bestplaces.net/religion/city/connecticut/shelton.

Hodara, Susan. "Living in Shelton, Conn.: More Living Space and Lower Taxes." *The New York Times*, March 17, 2021.
https://www.nytimes.com/2021/03/17/realestate/living-in-shelton-conn-more-space-lower-taxes.html.

Meeting Michael Bublé

Dictionary.com. s.v. "hari-kari." Accessed May 21, 2022.
https://www.dictionary.com/browse/hara-kiri.

Judge, Mike, dir. *Office Space*. 1999; Los Angeles, CA: 20th Century Fox, 2002. DVD.

That Moment in Amsterdam

Kenton, Will. "Clearing Prices." *Investopedia*, September 4, 2021.
https://www.investopedia.com/terms/c/clearingprice.asp#:~:text=The%20
market%20clearing%20price%20is,be%20produced%20at%20that%20price.

Bosses, Budgets and Bikinis

Moore, Jason, dir. *Pitch Perfect*. 2012; Universal City, CA: Universal Studios. DVD.

Studies Show, I'm an Asshole

Bemis, Thomas. "BMW Drivers Really Are Jerks, Studies Find." *Wall Street Journal MarketWatch*, August 13, 2013. https://www.marketwatch.com/video/bmw-drivers-really-are-jerks-studies-find/29285015-BB1A-4E41-B0C0-0A41CB990F60.html.

Elsom, Dan. "SMART CAR Why people who name and talk to their car are smarter than those who don't." *The Sun*, April 4, 2017. https://www.thesun.co.uk/motors/3253479/why-people-who-name-and-talk-to-their-car-are-smarter-than-those-who-dont/.

Through the Water Glass

Eliot, T.S. *Old Possum's Book of Practical Cats*. London: Faber and Faber, 1939.

Kept Women in Umbria

Hodara, Susan. "Living in Shelton, Conn.: More Living Space and Lower Taxes." *The New York Times*, March 17, 2021. https://www.nytimes.com/2021/03/17/realestate/living-in-shelton-conn-more-space-lower-taxes.html.

Rowling, J.K. *Harry Potter and the Order of the Phoenix*. New York, NY: Arthur A. Levine Books, 2003.

The Empath and the Sommelier

Google Dictionary. s.v. "empath." Accessed May 23, 2022. https://www.google.com/search?q=google+dictionary&oq=google+dictionary&aqs=chrome..69i57j0i512l4j0i131i433i512j0i433i512j0i512j0i433i512j0i512.5482j0j7&sourceid=chrome&ie=UTF-8#dobs=empath.

Orloff, Judith. "10 Traits Empathic People Share." *Psychology Today*, February 19, 2016. https://www.psychologytoday.com/us/blog/emotional-freedom/201602/10-traits-empathic-people-share.

Meet-Cute Meltdown

Mallet, David, dir. *Andrew Lloyd Webber's Cats*. 2005; Universal City, CA: Universal Pictures Home Entertainment. DVD.

Merriam-Webster Online. s.v. "meet-cute." Accessed May 21, 2022. https://www.merriam-webster.com/dictionary/meet-cute.

Meyers, Nancy, dir. *The Holiday*. 2006; Culver City, CA: Columbia Pictures, 2007. DVD.

Iceland: The (Christmas) Cat's Meow

Post Malone. "Circles." Republic, 2019, mp3 audio file.

About the Author

Sara E. Braca has always been curious about pretty much everything, which almost explains how she accidentally became a Renaissance woman living in a medieval Italian city. A graduate of Dartmouth College and Wharton, she is now a solo traveler, marketing executive, yoga instructor, cat mom, and wine enthusiast. Her passion for finding joy in her single life and empowering others to do the same drove her to add "debut memoirist" to this list. She lives in Tuscany.

For more information and a Reader's Guide to *When the Church Burns Down, Cancel the Wedding*, please visit sarabracaauthor.com.

9 798885 045988